To a
Thousand
Generations

Infant Baptism:
Covenant Mercy
for the People of God

Douglas Wilson

Canon Press

MOSCOW, IDAHO

Douglas Wilson, *To A Thousand Generations—Infant Baptism: Covenant Mercy for the People of God*

© 1996 by Douglas Wilson,
Published by Canon Press, P.O. Box 8741, Moscow, ID 83843

Cover design by Paige Atwood Design, Moscow, ID

Printed in the United States of America.

ISBN: 1-885767-08-0

Contents

Preface to the Reader

This small book is published by Canon Press, which is one of the literature ministries of Community Evangelical Fellowship in Moscow, Idaho. The subject of this book is infant baptism, a controversial subject in many churches.

As our church has worked through this issue practically, we have adopted a baptismal cooperation agreement, which for some years has enabled believers on both sides of this issue to work together harmoniously. We receive both baptistic and paedobaptistic households into membership. We practice both infant baptism and baptism upon profession of faith. We are able to do this because the membership of our church is reckoned by household, and because we all share a strong sense of the covenantal identity of each household, whether baptist or paedobaptist.

As a part of this cooperation agreement, we have stated the following in our Constitution: "Because of our commitment to the unity of the Spirit in the bond of peace (Eph. 4:3), and because of our shared commitment to the practice of household membership as outlined in our Constitution, these differences have been procedurally resolved between us. We have agreed to work together in this way until such time as the Lord brings us to one mind on the subject of baptism." Our assumption is that we are to *strive* for likemindedness. The cooperation is not based upon an uneasy silence, but rather on frank and charitable discussion.

Obviously, the publication of this book does not mean

that everyone associated with CEF agrees with the arguments contained here. Nevertheless, the elders of CEF have authorized the publication of this work, not because they all agree, but because of our shared commitment to remain in fellowship while we study the issue. The publication of this book invites you to study along with us.

Introduction

I must confess at the outset that this short book seeks to persuade others. The position maintained throughout the following pages is that there is a type of infant baptism which is thoroughly biblical, and which, when biblically *practiced*, adorns the gospel. But I am not seeking to persuade those who have no commitment to the teaching of Scripture, or those whose commitment is nominal. For such, there are many other topics, of a more important nature, which should be discussed first. Rather, I am addressing these comments to Christians who are serious about their faith, and who are also convinced that the practice of believer's baptism is the New Testament practice.

They are further convinced that believer's baptism is essential in guarding against the nominalism that has been the bane of genuine Christianity down through history. It must be admitted that infant baptism, as it has been administered by *some*, has been the point of stumbling for many professing Christians into a soul-destroying nominalism. But as we shall also see, nominalism afflicts baptist churches as well. The real origin of nominalism is to be found in all churches that refuse to *discipline* in terms of their baptism, whatever their practice of baptism may be.

Because evangelical baptists are my intended audience, I must begin with some background and disclaimers. I was baptized by immersion in a Christmas Eve service when I was ten-years-old in a Southern Baptist church. I grew up in a very godly home, and never had any cause to question my baptistic assumptions. When I was grown, through a series of providential circumstances I was called to a teaching/preaching ministry in an independent, evangelical baptistic church. In the course of ministering in this church over the years, I baptized many individuals—including my own three children. All that I baptized were professing believers.

During this time, my baptistic views were reinforced considerably, although I do not believe this was the result of mere repetition. One of the common features of many of the baptisms we performed was our practice of having those who were to be baptized give their testimonies if they so desired. One of the distressing features common to many of these testimonies was heard from individuals who had come to Christ in their mature years. They had already been baptized in infancy, and had grown up in a nominally Christian "churchy" kind of atmosphere. For many of them, despite all the church and more church, they were really clueless about the meaning and import of the saving gospel of Jesus Christ. That is, they did not understand the gospel until they came to a knowledge of Christ in a setting *unrelated* to their nominal upbringing. Receiving the gift of salvation meant, for these individuals, a virtual break with what they had previously been taught about the saving grace of our Lord Jesus Christ. I think it can be said safely that as long as this kind of tragic nominalism among paedobaptists exists anywhere, there will always be, in reaction, evangelical baptists. In fairness, however, it should be said again that nominalism is not the possession of paedobaptists alone. A baptist culture is also fully capable of bringing up children who embrace the form of religion, but deny the power. Many of those who are returning to the covenantal understanding of Reformed theology are doing so precisely because of the prevailing nominalism and superficiality of American baptist culture.

My desire is to present here a case for *biblical* infant baptism. This means, in part, that there is no intention whatever to defend the many forms of *unbiblical* infant baptism. Indeed, it is important for biblical paedobaptists to attack publicly the various errors that have grown up around the practice of infant baptism. No one thinks of accusing Southern Baptists of holding to baptismal regeneration, even though the Church of Christ (also immersionist and baptistic) does hold to it. In the same way, we need to get to the point where no one would dream of accusing an evangelical paedobaptist of holding to the false and destructive doctrine of baptismal regeneration—even though the Roman Catholic church does.

But in arguing for biblical infant baptism, it is not sufficient for us to say that infant baptism is merely *consistent* with the Scriptures, or that *a* biblical case can be made for it. In order for us to be satisfied that we are being biblical Christians, we must be content with nothing less than a clear biblical case *requiring* infant baptism. In a doctrinal matter of this importance, the standards of evidence are high.

Historically, the debate between baptists and covenantal paedobaptists has revolved around the two initiatory rites of circumcision and baptism, and has concerned how much continuity or discontinuity there is between the Levitical administration of the law and the New Covenant. But both sides agree that, at the very least, there is *some* discontinuity of administration. For example, girls as well as boys are baptized, and most paedobaptist churches do not require baptism eight days after birth. Consequently, the debate reduces to *how much* discontinuity there is between the rites. And because there appears to be no explicit baptism of an infant in the New Testament, the debate roars on unimpeded. After all, could not a covenantal shift to "believer's baptism" be seen and understood as an *administrative* change?

The debate should begin where the problem does—*with our children*. The issues addressed here should operate against the backdrop of the promises and duties of Christian parents, and the status of their children. Only after a theology of parenthood is understood may we properly turn to a discussion of covenantal baptism. When it comes to child-rearing, between the Old and New Testaments there is total and complete continuity *on the subject of godly parenting*. There is no discontinuity. It needs to be emphasized again that there is continuity *in the promises of God* with regard to *parenting*. Not surprisingly, this has ramifications for the subject of infant baptism. A detailed treatment of God's promises to parents can be found in my book *Standing on the Promises*. Due to limitations of space, those arguments will be repeated here but not in detail. Nevertheless, it is important for the reader to note that certain assumptions about the covenant of parenthood lie underneath this discussion of infant baptism, and for those who want to pursue that aspect of the question further, other material is available.

And now for some disclaimers. Perhaps at the outset I may be able to reassure the baptist reader by saying there will be no "babies of the Philippian jailer" arguments found in this book. Arguments from silence not only do *not* establish the point they seek to establish, they *do* help establish the reputation of paedobaptists in making desperate and valiant attempts to find *something* in the New Testament that teaches infant baptism. And besides, the youngest child of the Philippian jailor was a fourteen-year-old girl. ("And where did you get *that*?" "In the same verse where she was babysitting the three infants.") Although the general New Testament practice of household baptism is *related* to the subject of infant baptism (obviously), and will be discussed in its proper place later, arguments from such incidents are by no means a champion of the paedobaptist exegetical cause. At best, such arguments should be like Ephraim, helping to join in the pursuit later on.

So I have sought to avoid arguments that are merely *con-*

sistent with the practice of infant baptism. The goal of this small book is to demonstrate to evangelical baptists that infant baptism is biblically necessary, and such a task requires an approach that begins with *shared* or *indisputable* premises. Such an approach is being attempted in the following chapters. It is worth mentioning, however, that in the early sections of this essay the reader may wonder why the argument is not more compelling, and why there is not more water in view. ("I thought this was a book on *baptism!*") One of the problems in the entire debate over baptism has been the natural mistake of deriving the doctrine of the covenant from our doctrine of baptism, instead of beginning with the doctrine of the covenant, and then proceeding to discuss baptism. Many Christians have come to baptistic conclusions because they simply took a Bible and a concordance, and then looked up every incident of baptism in the New Testament. This is objectionable, not because they studied the passages concerned with baptism, but because they did *not* look up all the passages that addressed parents, children, generations, descendants, promises, covenants, circumcision, Gentiles, Jews, olive trees, and countless other important areas. In other words, the subject is bigger than it looks.

Another disclaimer is this. For evangelical baptists one of the hardest things to overcome in a discussion of these matters is the prejudice that associates *any* form of infant baptism with the kind of paedobaptism which is practiced, for example, by the Roman Catholic church. This is honestly one of the hardest aspects of the discussion for baptists to get past. But in the arguments that follow, there is no creeping sacerdotalism or advocacy of priestcraft *of any kind.* Biblically understood and practiced, infant baptism is thoroughly and completely evangelical.

Overcoming this prejudice is not really part of the debate, but it is something that must be addressed so that the discussion can proceed—this matter is quite a stumbling block. To an evangelical baptist, all forms of infant baptism *look* like Roman Catholicism, or like something that is headed there at a rapid clip. It therefore must be said with some emphasis and force that the arguments below are evangelical and covenantal, and *not* sacerdotal. To be explicit, all teaching that grace is somehow imparted to an infant *ex opere operato* (automatically, by some kind of ecclesiastical magic) is rejected here as sub-Christian (indeed, as will be seen, it is sub-Jewish), and detrimental to a faithful preaching of the gospel. Water baptism does not regenerate, it does not save, and it does not cleanse.

So why should we apply it to infants then? Now *that* is a good question.

1

Children of Believers as Members of the Kingdom

Members of the Kingdom

The Bible teaches that children of believers are members of the New Covenant. First, children of believers are expressly included in the prophecies of the coming New Covenant. Their ongoing inclusion throughout the prophecies is one of the great promised features of that glorious coming covenant. Jeremiah, the great prophet of the New Covenant, promises this. "They shall be *My people*, and I will be their God; then I will give them one heart and one way, that *they may fear Me forever*, for the good of them *and their children after them*. And I will make *an everlasting covenant* with them, that I will not turn away from doing them good; but I will put My fear in their hearts so that *they will not depart from Me*" (Jer. 32:38-40). Isaiah promises the same thing as an important feature of the New Covenant. "As for Me," says the LORD, "this is *My covenant* with them: *My Spirit* who is upon you, and *My words* which I have put in your mouth, *shall not depart* from your mouth, nor from the mouth of *your descendants*, nor from the mouth of your *descendants' descendants*," says the LORD, "from this time and *forevermore*" (Is. 59:21).

Ezekiel promises a glorious future too.

David My servant shall be king over them, and they shall all have one shepherd; they shall also walk in My judgments and observe My statutes, and do them. Then they shall dwell in the land that I have given to Jacob My servant, where your fathers dwelt; and they shall dwell there, *they, their children, and their children's children, forever;* and My servant David shall be their prince forever. Moreover I will make *a covenant of peace* with them, and it shall be *an everlasting covenant* with them; I will establish them and *multiply them*, and I will set My sanctuary in their midst forevermore" (Ez. 37:24-26).

We may confidently say that under the New Covenant, the children of believers are truly *included*. In Psalm 103, the psalmist predicts it clearly. "But the mercy of the Lord is from everlasting to everlasting on those who fear Him, and His righteousness *to children's children*, to such as keep *His covenant*, and to those who remember His commandments to do them" (Ps. 103:17-18). And Mary, the Lord's mother, quotes this psalmist. Her Son did not come to abrogate such promises. "For He has regarded the lowly state of His maidservant; for behold, henceforth all generations will call me blessed. For He who is mighty has done great things for me, and holy is His name. And His mercy is on those who fear Him *from generation to generation*" (Luke 1:48-50).

Given the context of these glorious promises (and many more), notice how Peter speaks to the Jews in the first sermon of the New Covenant, a sermon which cut the listeners to the heart. They cried out, seeking what they should do. Peter told them to repent and be *baptized*, and that the promise was to them *and to their children*. "For the *promise* is to you and to your *children*, and to all who are afar off, as many as the Lord our God will call" (Acts 2:39). Now the historical/grammatical approach to Scripture rightly requires us to seek to understand words as the first readers or listeners understood them. And how would Peter's listeners have heard him? Given his choice of words, what did Peter want them to think? Unlike many modern believers, they knew their Old Testaments. If anyone at that time had seriously maintained this meant the children of believers were now to be excluded unless they came into the covenant on their own as a separate individual, this would have been, in the first century, *an incomprehensible doctrine.* We must not come to the text of Scripture with our modern debates in the forefront of our mind. Our modern debates should be *settled* by Scripture, but this does not mean they are *found* in Scripture. The issue for us should be to learn what *their* debates were. And as the history of the church revealed in Acts shows, their central debate was over whether or not the Gentiles had to include their children in the New Covenant *by means of circumcision*—their debate was not whether the Jewish Christians had to start excluding their children.

Covenantal Parent/Child Relationship

The Bible teaches that one of the features of the New Covenant was to be the *restoration* of the covenantal parent/child relationship, not the *dissolution* of the covenantal parent/child relationship. "He will also go before Him in the spirit and power of Elijah, 'to turn the hearts of the fathers to the *children,*' and the disobedient to the wisdom of the just, *to make ready a people* prepared for the Lord" (Luke 1:17). The New Covenant has better promises (Heb. 8:6). But if such glorious *generational* and *covenantal* promises are ascribed to the Old Covenant, and are abandoned by the New, then how are the promises better? Under the Old Covenant, the children regularly fell into apostasy. But God promises that under the New Covenant, *this pattern will change.* If we forsake our covenant children, we are returning to the lifestyle seen under the powerless shadows, which could not maintain faithfulness over generations. The Old Covenant had its problems, not because it could successfully keep subsequent generations faithful to the covenant and within it, but because it could *not*. What a tragedy that modern Christians think this way: "For what the Old Covenant could not do in that it was weakened by the flesh, the New Covenant can't do either!"

The teaching of Scripture is very plain. Children of believers are members of Christ's kingdom. Little children and infants of believers are expressly included by Christ in the kingdom of *God*, in the kingdom of *heaven*. Jesus said this, "Let the *little children* come to *Me*, and do not forbid them; for *of such is the kingdom of heaven*" (Matt. 19:14; Mk. 10:14). And Luke gives us more information. "Then they also brought *infants* to Him that He might touch them; but when the disciples saw it, they rebuked them. But Jesus called them to Him and said, 'Let the *little children* come to Me, and do not forbid them; for *of such is the kingdom of God*'" (Luke 18:15-16). Luke here expressly names some of those brought to Christ as infants (*brephos*). Moreover, Jesus says that little children who are *brought* by another are little children who *come* to Him. It may be protested that there is no water, no baptism, in these passages. This is cheerfully acknowledged. We are not talking about baptism; we are talking about the relationship between Christ, His kingdom, and the infants and children of believers in Christ. Children *are* in the passage.

A Proper Criterion

Some still may be looking for an express warrant, or unambiguous example of an infant baptism in the New Testament. But this is a false criterion, which no one can consistently apply. For example, should women receive the Lord's Supper? After all, there is *no command* to give them the supper, and there is *no example* of them receiving the supper. The answer must be to appeal to a passage which has nothing to do with the Lord's Supper, but which has everything to do with the status of women in Christ's church. "There is neither Jew nor Greek, there is neither slave nor free, there is neither male nor female; for you are all one in Christ Jesus" (Gal. 3:28). This is an argument from the theological status of women (on which the New Testament is very clear) to the ordinance of the Lord's Supper (about which the New Testament says nothing in regard to women). This is a thoroughly biblical way of argumentation, and this is the method employed here as we consider the theological status of the *children of believers* as presented in the New Testament. We are arguing here from their status to the ordinance, from their standing to the sacrament. It may be protested that the blessing of the children just means that Christians are to be *like* children in their receptivity to the teaching of the kingdom. But Jesus teaches *elsewhere* that believers are to be like children. In this place, Jesus is teaching that children themselves are not to be kept away from Him.

Covenantally Holy

The New Testament recognizes that children of believers are holy ones or saints. We are taught that children of at least one believing parent are holy ones. This does not guarantee that each child is personally holy, but rather teaches that they are *federally holy*, or, put another way, *covenantally holy*. "For the unbelieving husband is sanctified by the wife, and the unbelieving wife is sanctified by the husband; otherwise *your children* would be *unclean*, but now they are *holy*" (1 Cor. 7:14). The word used by Paul is *hagia*, which when applied to *persons* is almost always translated *saint*. The "sanctification" of the unbelieving spouse is *so that* the descendants would be saints. It is a limited sanctification with a particular purpose in mind.

The New Testament also teaches Gentile children of believers that the covenant promise made at Sinai applies to them. "*Children*, obey your parents in the Lord, for this is right. 'Honor your father and mother,' which is the first commandment with *promise*: 'that it may be well with you and you may live long on the earth'" (Eph. 6:1-3). The commandments at Sinai were the terms of the *covenant*. "The Lord did not make *this covenant* with our fathers, but with us, those who are here today, all of us who are alive" (Dt. 5:3). Paul expands *the promise of this covenant* from the covenant children of the *land* to the covenant children of the *earth*. Gentile children are therefore included in the covenant.

Corporate Mindset

The baptist must assume that in the transition to the New Covenant, corporate nouns have changed their meaning. The paedobaptist assumes that corporate nouns have not changed their basic meaning in this transition to the New Covenant. For example, the gospel is for the *families* of the earth. "You are sons of the prophets, and of the *covenant* which God made with our fathers, saying to Abraham, 'And in your seed all the *families* of the earth shall be blessed'" (Acts 3:25). The gospel is for the *nations* of the earth. "Go therefore and make disciples of all the *nations*, *baptizing* them in the name of the Father and of the Son and of the Holy Spirit" (Matt. 28:19). The gospel is for the *households* of the earth.

> Now a certain woman named Lydia heard us. She was a seller of purple from the city of Thyatira, who worshiped God. The Lord opened her heart to heed the things spoken by Paul. And when she *and her household* were *baptized*, she begged us, saying, 'If you have judged me to be faithful to the Lord, come to my house and stay.' So she persuaded us' (Acts 16:14-15).

The point being made here is *not* that these are narratives of infant baptisms. The point is that they are narratives of *household* or *family* baptisms (1 Cor. 1:16). The gospel is for the *generations* of the earth. One of the most precious doctrines of

Scripture for believing parents is the teaching of *covenantal succession* from one generation to the next (Ps. 102:28). "They shall not labor in vain, nor bring forth children for trouble; for they shall be the descendants of the blessed of the Lord, *and their offspring with them*" (Is. 65:23). We are taught the same thing in Deuteronomy: "Therefore know that the Lord your God, He is God, the faithful God *who keeps covenant* and mercy *for a thousand generations* with those who love Him and keep His commandments" (Dt. 7:9). This corporate mindset, alien to the modern individualist, is simply taken for granted in Scripture.

Unregenerate Children

Now if children have this relationship to the people of God, then does it not follow that they are subjects of discipline? What happens when a child baptized in infancy grows to a point where it becomes apparent that he is in fact in rebellion against God? What should be done then? The exhibition of unregeneracy in a member is something which a paedobaptist church can and *must* address with church discipline. This should be so whether or not the person was baptized in infancy. The appearance of an "evil heart of unbelief" must be addressed as soon as it becomes apparent. But could not someone argue that since the church baptized the infant, *knowing* full well he was an individual non-confessor of Christ, then that church has no grounds to object when later the child continues to be that very same non-confessor of Christ?

The church should have baptized the infant with the stated expectation that the child must come to the Lord's Supper when he is able to discern the Lord's body (coming to the table is *not* optional), and that the child cannot discern the Lord's body without individual, confessed faith in the Lord. In a biblical paedobaptist church, if a baptized child grows up and refuses to profess his faith in the Lord Jesus, that child *must* be removed from the church. Why? Because it is gross sin for the elders of a church to tolerate members who are known to be in rebellion against God.

But how do we know someone to be unregenerate? The Bible gives us only one criterion—*fruit*, which is seen in the various works of the flesh. But infancy in a godly household is not a work of the flesh. The kingdom of heaven consists *of such*. When the scribes and Pharisees were disputing and arguing with their nation's Messiah, preparing to crucify Him, the little children were running around in the Temple, crying, "Hosanna to the son of David!" When Christ was told to rebuke them, He refused by quoting Psalm 8, saying, "Out of the mouths of *babes*." John the Baptist was filled with the Spirit before he was born, and *rejoiced* in Christ before he was born. The psalmist said that God made him to trust in God from his mother's breast.

This is not because little children are by nature innocent. They are not; they are all children of Adam and have inherited his sin. This is clearly seen in the children of unbelievers; they are expressly identified as *unclean* (1 Cor. 7:14). It is a strong word, commonly used to refer to demonic spirits; it means *foul*. This is what we all are by nature. But what has been given to us in the covenant of grace? The children of at least one believer are described as *holy ones*, or *saints* (1 Cor. 7:14).

If a church baptized someone *known* to be an unbeliever, it would be necessary to conclude the baptism service with the opening of procedures for excommunication. But it is obviously unscriptural to baptize someone who becomes at once an immediate candidate for church discipline. But someone is only a candidate for church discipline when his rebellion is *apparent*. It is not apparent in infants being brought up by godly parents.

2

Moses was a Christian

Covenantal Administrations

The phrase *Old Covenant* is found in only one place in Scripture. In 2 Corinthians, Paul, referring to the veil over the minds of the Jews in their hearing of the law, said this, "But their minds were blinded. For until this day the same veil remains unlifted in the reading of the Old Testament, because the veil is taken away in Christ" (2 Cor. 3:14). The word translated *Testament* here is *diatheke*, also reasonably translated as *covenant*. And there is one other place where the phrase may be legitimately inferred. "In that He says, 'A new covenant,' He has made the first obsolete. Now what is becoming obsolete and growing old is ready to vanish away" (Heb. 8:13). It is therefore proper to use the phrase *Old Covenant* in reference to the Levitical system of worship given to Moses. At the same time, there are great dangers; much of our understanding of the content of the phrase comes not from a careful exegesis of these two passages, but rather from the supposed and assumed antithesis it represents with the more common phrase *New Covenant*. Our common use of it therefore tends to obscure more than it reveals.

Promise, Law, Fulfilled Promise

As the issue of infant baptism is studied, it becomes clear that the issue of continuity between the Old and New Testament must also be understood and studied. As the study is undertaken, however, we must remember the transition from circumcision to baptism is not between something that originated in the Mosaic covenant and which was then carried over to the New Covenant. Circumcision began with the *promise*, to use Paul's terms, and not with the *law*. It is part of the promise to Abraham, and was not instituted at Sinai.

As Paul teaches us, the promise was first, and then came the law. This does not mean the law was a detour from the promise; rather it was the next step in the development and fulfillment of the promise. And as the New Testament makes so clear, the law serves the promise, and not the other way around.

At the same time, it is important for us to note the Bible's teaching on the relationship between the Levitical system and the New Covenant—between the law and the *fulfilled* promise. The order we see in Scripture is *promise, law, fulfilled promise*. So the law serves the promise, certainly, but in what way? What is the relationship between the Levitical administration of the Mosaic covenant and the New Covenant? What are the differences between them? The Bible details a number of very important distinctions; a careful examination of the differences will show them to be deep and *profound*.

Comparisons and Contrasts

First, the Bible teaches that the Levitical administration of the covenant was fleshly (Heb. 9:10); the New Covenant administration is spiritual (Heb. 9:11).

In describing the ordinances of the Old Covenant, the author of the book of Hebrews describes them as *fleshly*. By this he does not mean sinful or wicked, but he most certainly means that they are *material*—not spiritual—"concerned only with foods and drinks, various washings, and fleshly ordinances imposed until the time of reformation" (Heb. 9:10). In contrast to this, the New Covenant is spiritual. The next verse supplies the contrast. "But Christ came as High Priest of the good things to come" (Heb. 9:11a). The ordinances which were fleshly were replaced at the time of reformation—at the time of Christ's coming.

We also see that Scripture shows the Levitical administration of the covenant was glorious (2 Cor. 3:7-8); the New Covenant administration is far more glorious (2 Cor. 3:8-11).

Paul teaches us clearly that the ministry of Moses was a wonderful and a glorious thing. The glory involved was transient—but still glorious. It was glorious—but still transient: "but if the ministry of death, written and engraved on stones, was glorious, so that the children of Israel could not look steadily at the face of Moses because of the glory of his countenance, which glory was passing away" (2 Cor. 3:7). Paul goes on to show that the ministry of the New Covenant is possessed of a far greater glory. "How will the ministry of the Spirit not be more glorious? For if the ministry of condemnation had glory, the ministry of righteousness exceeds much more in glory. For even what was made glorious had no glory in this respect, because of the glory that excels. For if what is passing away was glorious, what remains is much more glorious" (2 Cor. 3:8-11).

Third, the Levitical administration of the covenant applied the law externally to stones (2 Cor. 3:3); the New Covenant administration applies the law internally to the heart (2 Cor. 3:3). When God gave the law to the people at Sinai, He did so by engraving the law on tablets of stone. The behavior of the people at the foot of the mountain while He was giving the law is ample demonstration that the law was not being engraved on their hearts: "clearly you are an epistle of Christ, ministered by us, written not with ink but by the Spirit of the living God, not on tablets of stone but on tablets of flesh, that is, of the heart" (2 Cor. 3:3). But under the New Covenant, God graciously places the law inside, in the hearts of His people.

The Bible also teaches that the Levitical administration of the covenant was temporary (Heb. 8:13); the New Covenant administration is permanent and eternal (Heb. 13:20).

"In that He says, 'A new covenant,' He has made the first obsolete. Now what is becoming obsolete and growing old is ready to vanish away" (Heb. 8:13). It would be hard for words to be more plain. The Levitical administration, at the time Hebrews was written, was "becoming obsolete" and "growing old" and ready to "vanish away." And in the judgment that fell on Jerusalem in 70 AD, we see the culmination of this. It *became* obsolete, it grew old and *died*, and has *vanished* away. The Levitical administration is no more. Contrast this with the everlasting nature of the New Covenant. "Now may the God of peace who brought up our Lord Jesus from the dead, that great Shepherd of the sheep, through the blood of the everlasting covenant" (Heb. 13:20). We are saved by the blood of the covenant, but it is not just "a" covenant. The blood was Christ's, and the covenant is eternal and everlasting.

We can see that the Levitical administration of the covenant was tangible (Heb. 12:18); the New Covenant administration is intangible (Heb. 12:22). "For you have not come to the mountain that may be touched and that burned with fire, and to blackness and darkness and tempest. . . . But you have come to Mount Zion and to the city of the living God, the heavenly Jerusalem, to an innumerable company of angels" (Heb. 12:18-22). The believers addressed in the book of Hebrews had not come to a physical mountain—Mt. Sinai. They had come to a heavenly mountain—the Zion above. The first mountain was tangible, and the people had to be warned against touching it. The latter mountain can only be touched *by faith*. It is far beyond the reach of human hands.

The Levitical administration of the covenant could not bring forgiveness to the conscience (Heb. 9:9-10); the New Covenant administration brings forgiveness to the conscience (Heb. 8:12). In describing the activity a believer went through under the Levitical system, the author of Hebrews takes great pains to point out what those gifts and sacrifices could not do. They could not cleanse the conscience. "It was symbolic for the present time in which both gifts and sacrifices are offered which cannot make him who performed the service perfect in regard to the conscience—concerned only with foods and drinks, various washings, and fleshly ordinances imposed until the time of reformation" (Heb. 9:9-10). A central feature of the New Covenant, however, was that it would do precisely that—cleanse the conscience. Quoting Jeremiah, the author of Hebrews assures us of the central importance of true forgiveness under the New Covenant. "For I will be merciful to their unrighteousness, and their sins and their lawless deeds I will remember no more" (Heb. 8:12).

Scripture teaches that the Levitical administration of the covenant could not bring compliance with the law (Rom. 8:3); the New Covenant administration effectuates compliance with the law (Rom. 8:3-4). It was not possible for a sinner to lift himself into obedience through attempted conformity to the law. This is because the law, being righteous, would only provoke the sinful heart into rebellion. The law could inform a sinner that he was a sinner, but the law could not make that sinner love righteousness. "For what the law could not do in that it was weak through the flesh, God did by sending His own Son in the likeness of sinful flesh, on account of sin: He condemned sin in the flesh, that the righteous requirement of the law might be fulfilled in us who do not walk according to the flesh but according to the Spirit" (Rom. 8:3-4). In contrast to this, what the law could not do, God did through sending His Son, the minister of the New Covenant. The law could not bring about obedience. But God brought about that missing obedience through sending His Son to be a sin offering—the sacrificed Lamb of the New Covenant.

The Levitical administration of the covenant culminated in a terrible curse for disobedience (2 Cor. 3:9); the New Covenant administration will culminate in a tremendous blessing for obedience (Heb. 8:11). Paul acknowledges the glory and goodness of the Levitical administration while at the same time showing how terrible it was for sinners—it was a ministry of condemnation. "For if the ministry of condemnation had glory, the ministry of righteousness exceeds much more in glory" (2 Cor. 3:9). The New Covenant will not end in the condemnation of the covenant people. Rather, it will end with a spotless bride, beautifully adorned for her Husband. The New Covenant is a ministry of worldwide salvation. It is efficacious, and the earth will be as full of the knowledge of the Lord as the waters cover the sea. "None of them shall teach his neighbor, and none his brother, saying, 'Know the Lord,' for all shall know Me, from the least of them to the greatest of them" (Heb. 8:11).

The Bible teaches the Levitical administration of the covenant was applied to the people of God in a condition of immaturity (Gal. 4:1-3); the New Covenant administration applies to the people of God in their majority (Gal. 4:4-7). "Now I say that the heir, as long as he is a child, does not differ at all from a slave, though he is master of all, but is under guardians and stewards until the time appointed by the father. Even so we, when we were children, were in bondage under the elements of the world. But when the fullness of the time had come, God sent forth His Son, born of a woman, born under the law, to redeem those who were under the law, that we might receive the adoption as sons. And because you are sons, God has sent forth the Spirit of His Son into your hearts, crying out, 'Abba, Father!' Therefore you are no longer a slave but a son, and if a son, then an heir of God through Christ" (Gal. 4:1-7).

There are two ways to apply this comparison, both of them valid and biblical. The first one is to point out that the child growing up and the child grown are the same child. The Israel of the Old Testament was Israel as a child. The New Israel of the New Testament is Israel matured. But our point here is the distinction between the Levitical administration and the New Covenant, and so that should be emphasized. The condition of the heir, when a child, *does not differ at all from a slave*. We are therefore justified in saying that under the Levitical administration the people of God lived in *servitude*—and it was a yoke that was impossible for them to bear (Acts 15:10). The people of God under the New Covenant are *free*—they have come into their promised inheritance. Although we have not received it fully (not having seen the redemption of the body), we have received enough of it to be *free*.

Scripture shows the Levitical administration of the covenant was of the letter (2 Cor. 3:6); the New Covenant administration is of the Spirit (2 Cor. 3:6). This contrast is another way of stating a point made earlier—the Levitical administration of the law is external, applied by the letter. The New Covenant applies the law internally, by means of the Spirit. "Not that we are sufficient of ourselves to think of anything as being from ourselves, but our sufficiency is from God, who also made us sufficient as ministers of the new covenant, not of the letter but of the Spirit; for the letter kills, but the Spirit gives life" (2 Cor. 3:5-6).

We can see the Levitical administration of the covenant spoke to men from earth (Heb. 12:25); the New Covenant administration speaks from heaven (Heb. 12:25). "See that you do not refuse Him who speaks. For if they did not escape who refused Him who spoke on earth, much more shall we not escape if we turn away from Him who speaks from heaven" (Heb. 12:25). The words spoken from God on earth were truly the words of God. Nevertheless, they were words of God spoken on earth. The condemnation of those who reject the words spoken from heaven will be much greater. They are sinning against a *much greater covenant*. The greatness of this covenant is seen in the source of the speaking of the words. The Levitical administration was spoken on earth, while the New Covenant is spoken from heaven.

The Bible shows the Levitical administration of the covenant was administered to the people through angels (Gal. 3:19; Acts 7: 35); the New Covenant administration is from God directly (Heb. 2:2-3). The author of Hebrews argues that this is one of the things that marks the superiority of the New Covenant. It is brought to the people *directly*. "For if the word spoken through angels proved steadfast, and every transgression and disobedience received a just reward, how shall we escape if we neglect so great a salvation, which at the first began to be spoken by the Lord, and was confirmed to us by those who heard Him" (Heb. 2:2-3). If those who rejected God's angelic messages of the law received condemnation, how much greater the condemnation will be for those who despise the blood and message of the New Covenant—a message spoken directly by Christ?

The Levitical administration brought strong curses for disobedience (Heb. 2:2-3); the New Covenant administration brings much greater curses (Heb. 10:29; 12:25). Christians commonly assume that the really terrifying curses for disobedience were given in the Old Testament, and that under the New Testament all is grace. But this is precisely the opposite of the New Testament's teaching on the subject. When the subject is addressed, we are reminded how much more we will be punished if we neglect this grace from heaven.

Now all the differences listed above certainly represent a tremendous contrast between the two covenantal administrations. But in reality, they are trifles compared with the greatest difference between the covenants. This final comparison is the one which reveals the greatest difference between the covenantal administrations, and yet, at the same time, shows the perfect harmony between them.

The Levitical administration of the covenant was an anticipation of a coming time of spiritual power (Jer. 31: 34); the New Covenant is powerful to save throughout all time, *including the time of the Levitical administration* (Heb. 9:15; John 8:58; Heb. 7:3). If the preceding truths concerning the Levitical administration were woodenly applied out of context, it could make us conclude that there was *no* true religion from the time of Moses to the time of Christ. Or possibly it could make us think, in agreement with some dispensationalism, that there was a different kind of religion in the Old Testament. Nevertheless, we know from Scripture that there were many faithful saints during that time, and that they were put right with God in the same way we are—by grace through faith. But how could such saints stand before God on the basis of a Levitical administration which was fleshly, earthly, temporary, immature, disobedient, cursed, external, *etc.*? A sinner needs far more than external religion in order to be able to stand before the Lord.

Faith in Christ

The answer is that they stood before God on the basis of the *gospel of Christ*, and they did so *by faith*. From Abel to Zechariah, and from John the Baptist down to the last sinner who will be brought into the kingdom before the End, we have all been saved by grace through faith. When the saints in the New Testament are being encouraged to stand in their faith, they are pointed to the great heroes of the faith throughout the *Old* Testament. Who are those saved by grace? Those who are of the seed of Abraham—those who believed just as he did. When are they saved by grace? They are saved down through human history, *whenever they believe.*

The author of Hebrews tells us this: "And for this reason He is the Mediator of the new covenant, by means of death, for the redemption of the transgressions under the first covenant, that those who are called may receive the promise of the eternal inheritance" (Heb. 9:15). In other words, the New Covenant is effective in the salvation of the Old Testament saints. How were David's sins washed away? *By the blood of Christ.* How was Abraham put right with God? *Through faith in the gospel.* But the blood of Christ is the blood of the New Covenant. And the gospel is the message of that same covenant. This is only possible because the New Covenant is *far greater* than the Levitical administration. The Levitical administration could not save retroactively; in fact, it could not save *at all.* It could only look forward in anticipation. The Christ of the New Covenant was savingly effective in the lives of Abraham, Samuel, David, and countless others. The second covenant not only saves those under the second covenant, it saves believers *under the first covenant.*

Preeminence of Christ

The writers of the New Testament had a tremendously high view of the New Covenant. In terms of it, they saw Christ *everywhere.* He, through the exaltation of the Father at the resurrection, was given preeminence over every name that can be named. But this glorious preeminence is seen by the New Testament writers in the history of the Old Testament, and not just after the birth of Christ. There are many examples of this perspective; perhaps just a few of the clearer ones will suffice.

Moses, we are told, made the right choice in throwing in his lot with the Israelites, instead of staying in his position of privilege at Pharaoh's court. But how does the author of Hebrews describe it? "By faith Moses, when he became of age, refused to be called the son of Pharaoh's daughter, choosing rather to suffer affliction with the people of God than to enjoy the passing pleasures of sin, esteeming the reproach of Christ greater riches than the treasures in Egypt; for he looked to the reward" (Heb. 11:24-26). Moses is described as choosing between the treasures of Egypt and the reproaches of *Christ*. What does this mean? He made the right choice; it means that Moses was a Christian. The fact that this sounds odd to us—*Moses?* a *Christian?*—simply shows how little we understand the tremendous authority Christ has under the New Covenant.

Paul tells about the experience with Christ the people of Israel had in the wilderness. He puts it this way: "Moreover, brethren, I do not want you to be unaware that all our fathers were under the cloud, all passed through the sea, all were baptized into Moses in the cloud and in the sea, all ate the same spiritual food, and all drank the same spiritual drink. For they drank of that spiritual Rock that followed them, and that Rock was Christ" (1 Cor. 10:1-4). The New Covenant is great indeed. The realities and saving blessings of the New Covenant pervade all of human history. After they were baptized into *Moses*, the people drank from *Christ*. The Levitical administration and the New Covenant are not placed end to end, with the New Covenant picking up where the Old Covenant left off. It is true that the New Covenant was formally inaugurated at the advent of Christ (*i.e.* manifested to the world), but, once inaugurated, the power and authority of the Christ of this covenant is seen by the New Testament writers *everywhere* in the world, and throughout *all time*.

A Temple of Living Stones

Consider the illustration of a great building. God has undertaken to build His Temple, and to do so out of living stones. He promised this building to Abraham, and told him what it would look like—He showed Abraham the blueprints, and Abraham *believed* the gospel in blueprint form. He knew that God would build the house just as He said He would. When the time came to begin the construction, the Lord brought His people up out of the land of Egypt—in fulfillment of His covenant promise to Abraham (Ex. 2:24). The construction process began in earnest. The giving of the law was preparation for the fulfilment of the promise.

Now at any building site, there are many materials used in the process of building that are not part of the final edifice. They are temporary; for an example, consider the scaffolding. When the building arrives at a certain point of completion, the scaffolding comes down.

Suppose, however, that in the process of building some of the workers became foolishly and emotionally attached to the scaffolding, and fought and resisted when the time came to take it down. What was their problem? They forgot the blueprints that had been in use from the first day of building—the blueprints that were shown to Abraham. Their resistance is overcome, however, and the scaffolding is removed. We then see the house promised to Abraham, and we understand that the scaffolding was a necessary part of the building process, but not a final part of the building. Furthermore, the scaffolding, when compared to the building as a building, *is far inferior to it.* Does this mean, Paul would ask, that the scaffolding was sin? Far from it—God required it; it was part of His perfect and revealed intention in the building of this house. The scaffolding *as scaffolding* is far superior to the building.

It would be a mistake to think that the scaffolding was intended to remain in place permanently as a part of the building. And it would be foolish to think that the scaffolding was another separate building entirely. And it would be yet another error to think the building was non-existent as long as the scaffolding stood—when the scaffolding came down there was nothing there until a building mysteriously appeared a short time later.

The writers of the New Testament look back and they always see the building—the house of Abraham, the house of Christ. The apostate Jews looked back and thought the scaffolding was the building. The Judaizers within the church thought the scaffolding was to remain permanently attached to the building. Extreme dispensationalists think the scaffolding was a separate outbuilding which God tore down, and will, in the very near future, rebuild for some reason. All these errors underestimate the authority Christ has in the New Covenant. There is a very common modern error among evangelicals which seems to exalt the authority of the New Covenant, but which in fact undercuts it. Many Christians assume that the power of the New Covenant is *limited* in extent, and has no retroactive authority. The New Covenant began at a certain point, the thinking goes, and has authority only from that point on.

But the glory of the New Covenant is that when Christ is seen by faith, and honored as Lord, the result is salvation. It does not matter when the faithful lived—pre or post scaffolding, or even if, like Abraham, they simply caught a glimpse of the blueprints.

Moses left Egypt to be with *Christ*. The people of Israel drank from the Rock that was *Christ*. They circumcised their children into *Christ*. But what of those who did not believe back then? What happened to them? The answer is the same thing that happens to those who commit the same sin now—their bodies are scattered over the wilderness. External religion never saved a soul, and has damned countless millions.

Our modern debates about infant baptism are not the result of the teaching of the text *directly*, but rather the result of the assumptions through which we see the text, and which govern our conclusions from the text. When we consider the ignominious history of unbelieving Jews throughout the Old Testament, why may baptists and paedobaptists express hearty agreement on the fact of this history, but then part company with one another on the theological *meaning* of that unbelief? There is no disagreement on the *fact* of their unbelief; we see disagreement on the *meaning* of that unbelief.

Unbelievers as Covenant Members

We should therefore understand the differing theological assumptions about the relationship of unbelief to the New Covenant. The baptistic assumption is that unbelief is utterly inconsistent with the New Covenant, such that the covenant cannot *really* be entered into by unbelievers. In other words, the sin of unbelief (to the point of apostasy) is an impossibility for members of the New Covenant. Therefore, the *elect* and the *covenant members* are the same set of people. The paedobaptistic assumption is that unbelief is utterly inconsistent with the New Covenant, such that it violates that covenant. Such a violation means that the curses of the covenant now apply to those unbelievers who are within the covenant. Therefore, the *elect* and the *covenant members* are not identical sets of people.

These two different assumptions are the result of disagreement about the similarity, or lack of it, between the Levitical covenant and the New Covenant *with regard to this one thing only*—the status of "covenant members" who are unbelievers at heart. The baptistic assumption is that the covenants are *unlike* in this respect. Some Old Covenant members were regenerate, some were not. All New Covenant members are regenerate. The paedobaptist assumption is that the covenants are *alike* in this respect. Some Old Covenant members were regenerate, some were not. Some New Covenant members are regenerate, some are not. The paedobaptist holds that the *difference* between the covenants is that the promises in the New are much better—meaning that the ratio of believer to unbeliever will drastically change. The history of the New Israel will not be dismal like the Old Israel.

So which set of assumptions is biblical? The teaching of the New Testament is that, *with respect to the possibility of covenant membership for those who are unbelievers in heart,* the covenant with the Jews and the covenant with the Christians are *alike.* Again and again, the New Testament sternly warns Christians against the same sin of unbelief which afflicted the Jews. "So we see that *they* could not enter in because of unbelief. Therefore, since a promise remains of entering His rest, let us fear lest any of *you* seem to have come short of it" (Heb. 3:19-4:1). And a chapter later, he says, "Let *us* therefore be diligent to enter that rest, lest *anyone* fall according to *the same example* of disobedience" (Heb. 4:11). This same theme comes up again later in the book. "Anyone who has rejected *Moses' law* dies without mercy on the testimony of two or three witnesses. Of how much *worse punishment*, do you suppose, will he be thought worthy who has trampled the Son of God underfoot, counted *the blood of the covenant by which he was sanctified* a common thing, and insulted the Spirit of grace?" (Heb. 10:28-29; cf. Heb. 2:1-3).

Paul teaches the same truth.

> Moreover, *brethren*, I do not want you to be unaware that *all our fathers* were under the cloud, all passed through the sea, all were *baptized* into Moses in the cloud and in the sea, all ate the same spiritual food, and all drank the same spiritual drink. For they drank of that spiritual Rock that followed them, and that Rock was Christ. *But with most of them God was not well pleased,* for their bodies were scattered

in the wilderness. Now these things became *our examples*, to the intent that *we should not lust* after evil things *as they also lusted*. And do not become idolaters *as were some of them*. As it is written, "The people sat down to eat and drink, and rose up to play." Nor let us commit sexual immorality, as some of them did, and in one day twenty-three thousand fell; *nor let us tempt Christ, as some of them also tempted*, and *were destroyed* by serpents; nor complain, as some of them also complained, and *were destroyed* by the destroyer. Now all these things happened to them as examples, and *they were written for our admonition*, upon whom the ends of the ages have come" (1 Cor. 10:1-11).

Paul's teaching in the book of Romans is the same. "Well said. Because of *unbelief* they were broken off, and *you stand by faith*. Do not be haughty, but fear. For if God did not spare the natural branches, *He may not spare you either*. Therefore consider the goodness and severity of God: on those who fell, severity; but toward you, goodness, *if* you continue in His goodness. Otherwise *you also* will be *cut off*" (Rom. 11:20-22). The Gentiles were threatened with removal from the *same tree* the unbelieving Jews had been in. But if this were the tree of salvation, then the elect can lose their salvation—which cannot be defended biblically. And if this is the tree of the covenant, then the point stands.

Therefore, confronted with the gross and unbelieving history of the Jews, the paedobaptist can tremble under the warnings of the New Covenant, which are great and terrible, and which teach us plainly that the same thing can befall *us*, and *will* befall us if we are not careful. At the same time, he can nonetheless take comfort with Paul in the promises of God, when he says, "What advantage then has the Jew, or *what is the profit of circumcision*? Much in every way! Chiefly because to them were committed the oracles of God. For what if *some* did not believe? Will their unbelief make the faithfulness of God without effect? Certainly not! Indeed, let God be true *but every man a liar*. As it is written: 'That You may be justified in Your words, and may overcome when You are judged'" (Rom. 3:1-4). Even though *some* Jews did not believe, Paul says that God remains faithful. Paul even goes on to say that even if *all* had not believed, God would still be true. If this were the case with the Old Covenant, then how much more is it true in the New?

Confronted with the gross and unbelieving history of the Jews, the baptist must say the Old Testament record of the disobedience of the Jews does *not* apply to our situation, and that to compare them is to compare apples and oranges. But this means he must therefore explain why the New Testament draws *parallels* where the baptist draws *contrasts*. The New Covenant warnings place Christians in the same place as the Jews *in this regard*. The Christian must "take heed lest he fall" in the same way they fell.

So what is meant by the author of Hebrews when he says that Christ is the Mediator of a *better* covenant established on *better* promises (Heb. 8:6)? How can it be better if the two covenants are part of the same covenantal history? Using scriptural examples, is the man better than the child he was? Is the harvest better than the planting? Is the pruned tree better than the overgrown tree? Is the house governed by the Son better than the house governed by the servant? *Of course*. And as we look at the promises concerning the effectual spread of the gospel throughout the earth, we look forward to the day when the New Covenant itself comes to a glorious maturity—and the bride will have no spot or wrinkle, and we will all know the Lord. The New Covenant will bring a much greater outpouring of efficacious glory from God than was previously seen in the world. More than that, as was shown, the New Covenant is so great that it is *retroactive*.

For now it is sufficient to say true religion has always been a matter of the heart. But in the latter days, the Lord has promised an effusion of the Spirit upon all flesh. The Levitical administration was for Israel in a condition of immaturity; it was entirely inadequate for the harvest of all nations.

The Bible teaches that true Jewishness, the kind of Jewishness available to all men through faith, is based on what the Spirit does in the heart of a man. "For he is not a Jew who is one outwardly, nor is that circumcision which is outward in the flesh; but he is a Jew who is one inwardly, and circumcision is that of the heart, in the Spirit, and not in the letter; whose praise is not from men but from God" (Rom. 2:28-9). In other words, if one's heart has been circumcised, then one is a true Jew, a true Israelite. Can a Gentile have a circumcised heart? Paul wrote this to the Colossians (a Gentile church): "In Him you were also circumcised with the circumcision made without hands" (Col. 2:11). Because their hearts were circumcised, they were true Israelites. But the heart circumcision of the Gentiles was done on the basis of the New Covenant—the covenant of maturity.

3

Circumcision and the Heart

Theological Relationship

God gave wonderful promises to believing parents prior to the coming of Christ. "'As for Me,' says the Lord, 'this is My covenant with them: My Spirit who is upon you, and My words which I have put in your mouth, shall not depart from your mouth, nor from the mouth of your descendants, nor from the mouth of your descendants' descendants,' says the Lord, 'from this time and forevermore'" (Is. 59:21). Following the advent of Christ, we have seen that these promises have not been altered in the slightest. The duties of parents *as parents* in both testaments clearly have been the same as well. This is all based upon the biblical constitution of the household, with the heart of that constitution being the covenantal relationship of a man to his wife. The marriage covenant is *always* a picture of Christ and the church, and has been so from the beginning. It will either be a lying picture or a true one, but a man and woman are always speaking of Christ.

Marriage is a covenant, and the children of believing unions are blessed and sanctified in both the Old and New Testament. "For the unbelieving husband is sanctified by the wife, and the unbelieving wife is sanctified by the husband; otherwise your children would be unclean, *but now they are holy*" (1

Cor. 7:14). This obviously relates to the question of the sign of the covenant, and whether or not it should be placed upon our children. But we must remember that we are coming to a subject upon which conscientious Christians disagree, and disagree strongly. This should not make us hesitate in presenting the truth, but we must at least recall that in discussing the sign of the covenant we are addressing the least important thing about it. Which is greater? The gold on the altar, or the altar which sanctifies the gold? Which is greater? The sign of the covenant, or the covenant itself? Those who are visible saints together with us are to be loved for the sake of Jesus Christ, whether or not we believe them to be mistaken on the question of the "water that divides."

The disagreement of Christians notwithstanding, the Scriptures very definitely connect the two signs of circumcision and baptism, which means that we must do the same. Therefore in this section, we shall look at the meaning of circumcision in some detail, and then look at the theological relationship between circumcision and baptism. As we proceed, these signs of God's covenant with His people must be held up against the backdrop of the promises and duties given to parents in both testaments. The authority of a faithful head of the household is not changed between the testaments; a man can still legitimately say, "As for me and my house, we will serve the Lord." This is possible because the Lord of the New Covenant saves *parents*, not isolated individuals, throughout human history.

In Genesis 17, the Lord appeared to Abram and made an *everlasting* covenant with him. God changed Abram's name to Abraham at this time, and promised the land of Canaan to Abraham's descendants as "an everlasting possession." In order for Abraham and his descendants to maintain this covenant, they were commanded, among other things, to practice circumcision. If circumcision was not performed, the covenant was broken (v. 14). In verse 11, the Lord stated that circumcision is "the sign of the covenant between me and you." Here we learn that physical circumcision was *a sign*. We know from this passage in Genesis that circumcision at least signified the covenant concerning the land of Canaan. However, was circumcision a sign that pointed to anything deeper than a promise of mere territory? Was Abraham justified simply because he realized that *real estate* is from the Lord? The New Testament answers this question unambiguously. Abraham was *not* concerned principally with Canaan. That land was merely a shadow of what was really promised to him, and he knew it. Paul tells us that Abraham had the *gospel* preached to him (Gal. 3:8), Christ tells us that Abraham looked forward in faith to the day of Christ, rejoiced to see it and was glad (John 8:56), and the author of Hebrews states in the plainest terms that:

> These all [including Abraham] died in faith, not having received the promises, but having seen them afar off were assured of them, embraced them and confessed that they were strangers and pilgrims on the earth. For those who say such things declare plainly that they seek a homeland. And truly if they had called to mind that country from which they had come out, they would have had opportunity to return. But now they desire a better, that is, a heavenly country. Therefore God is not ashamed to be called their God, for He has prepared a city for them (Heb. 11:13-16).

In other words, Abraham was promised the city of God, the redemption of all mankind, in the figure of Canaan, and he understood that figure. He was promised a redeemed world (Rom. 4:13). He truly was a great man of faith, and Christians are repeatedly called to imitate him. But we cannot imitate him without true faith, which means we must understand the types, figures and signs of the Old Testament *as he did*. We must see these types as having a thorough-going *evangelical* and *eschatological* significance.

Heart Circumcision

In Deuteronomy 10, Moses gave the people some instructions on possessing the land (Dt. 10:11-22). In verse 11, God commanded them to take the land. In verses 12-22, the Lord spoke concerning the heart attitude of the people as they occupied the land. In verse 16 they were commanded, "Therefore circumcise the foreskin of your heart, and be stiff-necked no longer." We see here that what God truly required of them was a circumcised *heart*, a heart that had stiff-necked rebelliousness removed. If the covenant between God and Israel was to be kept, then it would have to be kept on the spiritual level—not just externally kept by nominal Jews. Nominal Jews were faithless Jews, which meant that they were really not Jews at all. The covenant could not be faithfully kept by unregenerate men.

Thus, on one level, the sign of the covenant did signify the promise concerning Canaan. However, of necessity, it also signified the heart condition that would make the keeping of this external covenant possible. Simply stated, physical circumcision was given as a sign of *Christ*—who is the objective basis for spiritual or heart circumcision. The need for such a heart change is referred to in Jeremiah 4:4 where the prophet says, "Circumcise yourselves to the Lord, and take away the foreskins of your hearts." God placed a spiritual value on physical circumcision only so far as it represented a circumcised heart (cf. Jer. 9:25-26). As a sign, circumcision was external. But as a sign, it was also given to point to spiritual realities. But if we ask for a more detailed theological understanding of what a circumcised heart *is*, we shall have to turn to the New Testament for the answers.

In Romans 2:28-29, Paul expressly teaches that true circumcision is an internal matter; consequently, it is something that can only be performed by the Spirit of God. "For he is not a Jew who is one outwardly, nor is that circumcision which is outward in the flesh; but he is a Jew who is one inwardly, and circumcision is that of the heart, in the Spirit, and not in the letter; whose praise is not from men but from God." Paul is not primarily concerned with the external sign; he is concerned with the internal reality—a circumcised heart. This circumcision of the heart is described as the operation of the Spirit of God, which has to be understood as regeneration. It is the new birth which makes a true Jew. This is why it was so astonishing to Christ that a teacher of Israel did not know what He was talking about when He referred to the birth given by the Spirit (John 3). This was a truth taught plainly in the *Old* Testament Scriptures.

Two chapters later in Romans, Paul confirms what was said earlier about Abraham's circumcision. Circumcision was not given to Abraham as a security or earnest payment on the land of Canaan only. In Romans 4 Paul states

> Does this blessedness then come upon the circumcised only, or upon the uncircumcised also? For we say that faith was accounted to Abraham for righteousness. How then was it accounted? While he was circumcised, or uncircumcised? Not while circumcised, but while uncircumcised. And he received the sign of circumcision, a seal of the righteousness of the faith which he had while still uncircumcised, that he might be the father of all those who believe, though they are uncircumcised, that righteousness might be imputed to them also. . . . (Rom. 4:9-11).

Significance of Circumcision

It would be hard for Paul to make his point any more clearly. Abraham was declared righteous in the eyes of God *through his faith.* Abraham then received the sign of that righteousness, circumcision. Thus, we see that when Abraham was declared righteous by God, his heart was circumcised. Years later, he was physically circumcised as a sign. Paul says that Abraham received the *sign* of circumcision, which was also a *seal* of the righteousness he had by faith. This was a seal, *not of Abraham's faith*, but of the righteousness which he had *by* faith. Abraham's righteousness was not his own personal faith; his righteousness was Christ, whom he appropriated *by* faith. Thus, *the seal of circumcision was not a seal given as a personal testimony.* The seal was God's seal of the promised and coming Christ, in whom Abraham believed. The meaning of Abraham's circumcision was not, "Abraham got saved." Rather, it was, "Salvation will come to the world!" It is true that Abraham was personally saved, and that he was saved by faith. But he was saved because he believed in the objective promise—that is, in the coming Christ.

This is really quite important, because our tendency is to think that the seal is of something entirely subjective (personal faith) rather than objective (the saving Christ). Therefore, we think nothing can be sealed unless we have ascertained with our own eyes that it may be sealed. This means, we think, that we should not circumcise or baptize anyone until we can guarantee that they have professed faith and evidenced the true fruit of it. We baptize by sight, and not by faith.

But God commanded Abraham to circumcise both Isaac and Ishmael, *i.e.* to place the same sign and seal on them. What did *their* circumcision signify? Obviously, the same thing—it was a *sign* of the covenant between God and Abraham (and Abraham's seed). Now was it also a seal of *their* righteousness which *they* had by faith? Depending upon whether we are considering Isaac or Ishamael, the answer is *yes* and *no*. We see the same with Jacob and Esau. It was, on both of them, a seal of the coming Christ, the coming Righteousness. The mean-

ing of the sign and seal remained the same. But Jacob personally came to this righteousness of faith and Esau did not. Thus
Esau bore the seal of "the righteousness of *another*" hypocritically. The Jews who persecuted the Christ were following in
Esau's footsteps. They thought circumcision was a sign and
seal of *their own* righteousness. But it was not—it was a sign of
a covenant made with *sinners*, and a seal of a Righteousness
found in *Another*. The seal of circumcision was a seal of "the
Lord our Righteousness." We must always reject the natural
tendency to make the covenantal signs into a seal of our own
personal righteousness.

Remember that Paul is seeking to show how the physically uncircumcised Gentiles can consider Abraham for their
father—after all, he argues, Abraham's righteousness by faith
was evident *before* his physical circumcision. And of course,
his righteousness by faith was not ended by his circumcision
either—he was the father of *all* who believe, whether circumcised or uncircumcised. Further, he was never the father of
those who never believed, whether or not they had been physically circumcised.

This means that the blessedness promised to Abraham
came upon those circumcised in infancy, who later believed.
Abraham was their father. And if they were circumcised in
infancy but did not come to faith, he was not their father, and
they were not true Jews. Moreover, Abraham was the father
of *all* who believed, both Jew and Gentile. He bore in his
body, as did every circumcised Jew after him, the seal of the
coming Christ. This Christ was the Righteousness of uncircumcised and circumcised *both*. The blessing of Abraham did
not come upon the believing circumcised *only*.

This truth is seen again in Galatians 5:6, "For in Christ
Jesus neither circumcision nor uncircumcision avails anything,
but faith working through love." Paul is not concerned with
the flesh; he cares about the state of the heart, and whether

that heart has looked in faith to the Christ of history. It is Christ crucified, buried, and resurrected, under the administration of Pontius Pilate, who saves, and not a Christ-consciousness within the soul. The man who looks *out* is justified within. The man who looks in has lost himself in the deepest hell possible.

State of the Heart

It is of course true that real religion is concerned with the state of the heart, and not with whether a man has jumped through all the right ceremonial hoops. When a man believes the covenant promise he points away from himself. In the same way, the signs of that covenant point away from the redeemed and to the Redeemer. To look away from the heart to an objective Christ is not to neglect the heart; to look away in this fashion is the only way to be justified and put right with God.

Under the economy of the Levitical administration, if a man came to true faith, as did Abraham, then his circumcision was a sign and seal of the covenant which promised Christ, just as it had been with Abraham. This is so even though most of these believers had received the sign in infancy. And if a man never came to faith, his circumcision was nevertheless a sign and seal of Christ, and, because he bore the sign and seal hypocritically, it did nothing but increase his condemnation. Now when a Jew came to personal faith, given the nature of the case, recircumcision was not required (indeed, it was not even possible). His circumcision received in infancy was the sign and seal of Christ, who was now his by faith. If he grew up and was unfaithful to the terms of the covenant, the signification of circumcision did not therefore change. It was the fact that the signification did *not* change which made it possible for the prophets to cast the periodic hypocrisy of the Israelites into their teeth. "*You* are circumcised. But why is your *heart* not circumcised?"

So for those who came to faith, circumcision was a sign and seal of Righteousness by faith, just as it had been for Abraham. It was not a sign and seal of their *own* righteousness. For those who grew up in the covenant community, but who never came to saving faith, their circumcision was a sign of Righteousness by faith, and a seal of the coming Christ, in whom they refused to believe. And because they bore this sign hypocritically, preaching something they did not believe, their judgment was more severe. As the apostles and prophets made plain, to whom much is given, much is required.

4

Application to Baptism

Christ is the Message

How then does circumcision relate to baptism? Just as circumcision was a sign and seal of the Christ who was *to come*, so baptism is a sign and seal of the Christ who *came*. Circumcision looked forward in history, and Christian baptism looks back in history, but they both testify to the same Christ, the same Lord of the Covenant. Neither circumcision nor baptism primarily testifies concerning the inward state of the individual who bears the sign and seal; they testify of *Christ*.

Does not the state of the individual matter? Of course in one sense it matters very much. If a man bears the sign of Christ with hypocrisy, if he bears it in unbelief, he is incapable of speaking truthfully from the heart about *Christ*. His testimony is therefore obnoxious to God. He is not lying about his internal condition; his internal condition means he is lying about Christ.

So we err if we simply say that the external sign is a sign of internal spiritual realities within the individual, and stop there. It is true that when a person is a believer, the external sign does conform with these internal spiritual realities. But what *are* these realities? Regeneration? Christ is our Regeneration. Redemption? Christ is our Redemption. Forgiveness? Christ is our Forgiveness. The signs of the covenant acknowledge the objective ground of the covenant—the righteousness of the Lord Jesus Christ. These signs of circumcision and baptism are not arrows pointing *subjectively* to the redeemed man, they are arrows pointing *objectively* to the Redeemer.

The inward presence or absence of true faith is therefore crucial. The presence of true faith in the one baptized means that this particular messenger is faithful, but the faithfulness of the messenger cannot be the message. *Christ* is the message.

Not Done With Hands

With this in mind we may turn to see how Scripture connects the meaning of circumcision and baptism. Paul says this in Colossians 2:11-12: "In Him you were also circumcised with the circumcision made without hands, by putting off the body of the sins of the flesh, by the circumcision of Christ, buried with Him in baptism, in which you also were raised with Him through faith in the working of God, who raised Him from the dead." We learn several striking things from this passage. One is that Christians in Colossae (who were Gentiles and therefore physically uncircumcised) had been spiritually circumcised with the circumcision of Christ. In other words, the Christ *represented* by physical circumcision had circumcised their hearts so they could testify of Him in truth. Without having the external sign of circumcision, their heart circumcision testified of Christ.

Secondly, this spiritual circumcision was accomplished by means of burial with Christ *in baptism*. This is the connection between circumcision and baptism we are looking for. *There is a baptism which accomplishes the circumcision of Christ.* A baptism exists which accomplishes the putting off of the sins of the flesh. As Paul makes clear, this heart circumcision is not done *with hands*. This not only rules out physical circumcision, it rules out water baptism as well, both of which are performed by human hands. This is something deeper; it is a work of God in the heart. This heart circumcision is not accomplished by the external performance of *any* physical rite or ceremony, under any covenant.

The Same Spiritual Truth

But if it is not water baptism that accomplishes this, then what baptism is it? We learn in this passage that it is the baptism which buried us together *with Christ*. This baptism is referred to elsewhere. In Romans 6:3-4, Paul says to the Romans: "Or do you not know that as many of us as were baptized into Christ Jesus were baptized into His death? Therefore we were buried with Him through baptism into death, that just as Christ was raised from the dead by the glory of the Father, even so we also should walk in newness of life" (cf. Mk. 10:38; Lk. 12:50). It is here that we learn how *both* physical circumcision and water baptism are pictures of the *same spiritual truth*. In the Colossians passage, circumcision provides us with a picture of the removal of the "body of the sins of the flesh"—the work of Christ. Just as the foreskin is cut off and thrown away, the dominion of the flesh is completely removed from the life of anyone who is born again. In Romans 6, baptism pictures the burial of the old man. This old man is crucified in the work of Christ and is buried with Him. Baptism signifies this burial. Paul then goes on to say that our union with Christ does not end with the burial, but continues as we are raised to new life in the power of His resurrection.

The reality that both pictures signify is this: *the death of the old man in the cross of Christ*. Remember that this death is accomplished objectively in the cross by the death of *Christ*. We were baptized into *His* death. Circumcision points to a once-for-all separation from sin through surgery. Baptism points to a once-for-all separation from sin through death, burial, and resurrection. In both cases, the believer is freed from sin and has been given a glorious picture of that freedom. But this Freedom has a name, and His name is the Lord Jesus. It is important to reiterate that water baptism is not a picture of the believer's own personal death, burial and resurrection. It is a sign of the believer's union with and in the death, burial, and resurrection of *Another*.

An essential part of the argument in Romans 6 deals with the *union* of the believer with *Christ*. Paul mentions this same point in connection with baptism in Galatians 3:26-27: "For you are all sons of God through faith in Christ Jesus. For as many of you as were baptized into Christ have put on Christ." This true baptism may be called *a baptism of union*. The union is with Christ, and the effects of it are eternal. How is this baptism accomplished? In 1 Corinthians 12:13 it gives an answer: "For by one Spirit we were all baptized into one body— whether Jews or Greeks, whether slaves or free—and have all been made to drink into one Spirit." In this verse, Paul says that we are baptized *into a body*. Contextually, that body is the body of Christ. The Person who does the baptizing is the Holy Spirit. Just as an elder baptizes into water, so the Holy Spirit baptizes into Christ. And water baptism points to that baptism into *Christ*. The baptism of union with Christ is performed by the Spirit of God.

We saw earlier the Spirit's involvement in heart circumcision in Romans 2:29. There it refers to the *circumcision of the heart, by the Spirit*—the Holy Spirit (not man) performs true circumcision, which is the circumcision of the heart. The Holy Spirit (not man) performs true baptism, which is the baptism of the heart. This means we have established two things thus far concerning circumcision and baptism. Both of the external signs refer unambiguously to the Righteousness of Another, and the internal realties which keep the testimony from hypocrisy are brought about by the Spirit of God.

5

Water and Spirit

The Connection

We have seen that true circumcision is inward—it is circumcision of the heart. When faithfully understood by believing Jews, physical circumcision was a sign and seal of the Christ, who alone could provide salvation. When the sign was distorted by unbelief, the signification of circumcision remained, but it remained as the Song of Moses did—as a testimony against the one who bore the sign and seal in hypocrisy. We have also seen there is a true baptism which is identified with the true circumcision. That to which physical circumcision pointed was accomplished *for Gentiles* in Christ, and their baptism in water pointed to the same Savior.

But we still need to establish that water baptism is connected to the baptism of the Spirit. First, it is necessary to recall what this *spiritual baptism* of the Spirit accomplishes. It circumcises the heart by removing the body of fleshly sin. It places the individual in union with Christ in His death, burial, and resurrection. It washes all his sins away. In short, this true baptism is what makes a person regenerate. The baptism of the Spirit is not an experience subsequent to conversion, *it happens at conversion.*

With this understanding, we can turn to Acts 10. Peter

was preaching to Cornelius and his friends when the Holy Spirit fell on them all, bringing new life in Christ. They became regenerate. In verse 47, Peter says, "Can anyone forbid water, that these should not be baptized who have received the Holy Spirit just as we have?" And he commanded them to be baptized in the name of the Lord." These people have just become Christians. They have just had their initial encounter with the Spirit of God. Peter sees this *and cites it as his reason* for commanding that they be baptized with water. There is a clear and obvious connection between the baptism of the Spirit here and the baptism of water. Now some may argue that the passage does not refer to the baptism of the Spirit, but rather to *receiving* the Spirit. However, in the next chapter, when Peter is defending himself in Jerusalem, he connects the incident in Caesarea with the experience the disciples had at Pentecost in Jerusalem. He states in verse 15ff.: "And as I began to speak, the Holy Spirit fell upon them, as upon us at the beginning. Then I remembered the word of the Lord, how He said, 'John indeed baptized with water, but you shall be baptized with the Holy Spirit.' If therefore God gave them the same gift as He gave us when we believed on the Lord Jesus Christ, who was I that I could withstand God?" (Acts 11:15-17) It is clear that Cornelius, his family, and friends were baptized with the Holy Spirit, just as the disciples had been at Pentecost. Because God had clearly brought salvation to them, by means of the Spirit, Peter commanded water baptism. This means that we can now assert the connection between the baptism of the Spirit, and the baptism of water. We know that the latter corresponds with the former. The latter was given by Peter because the former was granted by God.

The Real Issue

But at this point could not a baptist object, and say that this is precisely his point? Did not Peter command water baptism because he saw that the Spirit had already baptised them? Does this not mean that we should wait until someone is converted by the Spirit before we offer water baptism? And does this not exclude infant baptism? But this objection misses the point that Peter is making. The issue with Cornelius and his household was not whether they were *old enough* to receive water baptism, but whether they were *Jewish* enough. If this household had contained an infant, the members of the "circumcision" who were there would not have objected to baptism on the grounds of infancy, but rather because the infant was *Gentile* and uncircumcised.

Nevertheless, we see in this passage that there is a clear connection between the baptism of the Spirit and baptism with water. This means that water baptism and physical circumcision are a sign of the same Christ, who brings the same salvation to all who believe on Him. Water baptism corresponds with heart circumcision, and physical circumcision corresponds with spiritual baptism. The external signs are therefore theologically equivalent signs—they point to the same Christ.

Thus, by way of summary, we can say that water baptism is related to Christ in three basic ways. First, it is connected to the circumcision of the heart. Second, it refers to the union of the believer with his Lord. This union includes identification with His righteousness, and with His death, burial and resurrection. Third, it is clearly related to the baptism of the Holy Spirit. Physical circumcision has the same relationship in all three respects, and was nonetheless administered to infants. There is therefore no compelling reason why Christians should not baptize the infants of believing parents as well.

What Water Baptism is Not

On the basis of what has been established already, we can say that water baptism is not sacred in itself; it *signifies* a holy Christ.

It is not an automatic means of imparting grace, it is a sign of grace that has been proclaimed and displayed in the covenant of grace. It is not a means of removing sins, but shows that the Spirit can wash cleaner than the purest water. In other words, water baptism is *not* a part of the gospel. It accompanies the gospel as a sign. And as such a sign, it displays the same essential things that were displayed by circumcision under the economy given to Abraham. And all those things find their center in Christ.

In 1 Corinthians 1:17, Paul makes a special effort to show that water baptism is not to be included as a part of the gospel. "For Christ did not send me to baptize, but to preach the gospel, not with wisdom of words, lest the cross of Christ should be made of no effect" (1 Cor. 1:17). But Christ *had* sent him to: "open their eyes, in order to turn them from darkness to light, and from the power of Satan to God, that they may receive forgiveness of sins and an inheritance among those who are sanctified by faith in Me" (Acts 26:18). Obviously it is possible to be forgiven and sanctified before undergoing water baptism (just as Abraham was forgiven and sanctified before he was circumcised). Christ sent Paul to preach this repentance, forgiveness, and sanctification. But Christ did *not* send Paul to baptize in water. Therefore, considered in itself, water baptism does not accomplish true forgiveness or sanctification.

An Antitype

Peter makes a similar distinction when he says: "There is also an antitype which now saves us—baptism (not the removal of the filth of the flesh, but the answer of a good conscience toward God), through the resurrection of Jesus Christ" (1 Peter 3:21). Peter makes a plain statement that it is not the physical water which has the saving effect ("*not* the removal of the filth of the flesh"). Salvation is accomplished by the resurrection of Jesus and our union with Him. As we saw earlier, this union is brought about by another baptism, the baptism of the Spirit. It is interesting to note that Peter describes baptism here as an *antitype*—the fulfillment of a *type* in the Old Testament. That Old Testament type was the flood at the time of Noah—God's judgment upon the sin of the antediluvians, and His salvation of Noah *and his household*. Christian baptism, Peter says, is typified in the Old Testament, but it is not to be considered as something magical or automatic. After all, Noah was in the ark, along with his family, because of his *faith*. In the same way, we come to Christian baptism on the basis of our faith in the resurrection of Jesus Christ.

Consequently, we are never to look for salvation in mere externals like physical circumcision or water baptism. We cannot manipulate Him through the things that we can do on the outside. The Lord is sovereign in salvation. From the time of Abraham until now, it has been clear that only *He* changes the one thing needful—He takes away the heart of stone and gives us a heart of flesh. And as our sovereign Lord, He places the sign of His covenant on us, and commands us to believe.

6

Circumcision in the New Covenant

Same Promises, Same Duties

Having established the groundwork, we now come to the point where we are ready to argue explicitly for the biblical practice of infant baptism as seen in the New Testament. Now we know the promises of God to parents are completely consistent throughout all of Scripture. The advent of the New Covenant does not establish a sudden insecurity in the minds of believing faithful parents. And further, we know the promises of God do not vary as they apply to Jew and Gentile parents. Because one of the most striking features of the New Covenant is the inclusion of Gentiles on a large scale, it is important to note that the promises of God to parents do not change as a result of this new state of affairs.

Nor does the fulfillment of God's covenant promises in Christ alter or change the *duties* of believing parents with regard to the rearing of their offspring. In short, in all eras, God commands parents to bring children up with Him as their God, and He promises that such a faithful upbringing will not be futile. And Scripture is consistently clear that the duties of godly parenthood are not altered if the parents are Gentile. Our pattern is to be that of Timothy's mother, Eunice, a woman of genuine faith, married to a pagan Gentile, who taught Timothy the Scriptures from infancy. "But you must continue in the things which you have learned and been assured of, knowing from whom you have learned them, and that from childhood you have known the Holy Scriptures, which are able to make you wise for salvation through faith which is in Christ Jesus" (2 Tim. 3:14-15). The word translated *childhood* here needs to be rendered *infancy.* Timothy had been brought up in the Scriptures from the very beginning. So the promises of God to parents are good, and the duties are clear. The structure underneath these promises, commands and duties, according to the Scriptures, is a covenantal structure—the structure of the covenant of redemption. We have been talking about the heart of this covenant as it applies to parenthood. With this in mind, we come now to the *sign* of that covenant.

The Sign of the New Covenant

The sign of initiation into the covenant was circumcision (beginning with Abraham); the rite of initiation became baptism with the advent of the New Covenant. The debate between baptists and paedobaptists concerns how much was kept or lost in that transfer. If the *mode* changed so drastically, could not the *subjects* of baptism drastically change as well?

As we begin to discuss the sign of the covenant, and whether Christian parents should baptize their infants, we must keep our perspective concerning what has true importance in these matters. As Scripture teaches from first to last, keeping the *covenant* is more important than externally keeping the *sign* of the covenant. Of course, as Christians we should always seek faithfully to do both, but on this subject especially we must remember what is the most important. Remembering this will enable baptists and paedobaptists to maintain a spirit of unity as they work through, debate, and discuss these issues.

We must rephrase the question of infant baptism. It is commonly said by baptists that no examples of "infant baptism" are in the New Testament, or are required by the New Testament. I ought to know that this is the case; I have said something like it often enough myself. And it certainly looks this way at first glance—although the claim is too easily made, and too infrequently challenged. When it *is* challenged, it is challenged with inadequate arguments from silence—the purported babies of the Philippian jailer being one example. If we only produce examples in the New Testament where *maybe* they baptized infants, we may legitimately conclude that *maybe* we should too. This is hardly a solid foundation upon which to build a basic parental Christian duty—if duty it is. All too often paedobaptists grant that the New Testament offers no examples of infant baptism, and then seek to establish their case on grounds of continuity with the Old Testament. Continuity from the Old Testament does provide a strong and compelling case, but it is often assumed on all hands that the New Testament is silent on this.

New Testament Examples

But *does* the New Testament provide no examples of infant baptism? Let us begin our consideration of this whole question from another angle. Suppose we start by phrasing the first question we ask a little differently. Suppose we ask it in this way. *In the New Testament, do any Christian parents place upon their infants a covenantal sign of their identification with Christ? If they do, does the practice have apostolic sanction?* The answer to these questions is an emphatic *yes*. Notice that the questions are not asking about the Old Testament era. Phrased in this way, we are asking the question about *Christian* parents, who are living under the *New* Covenant. In Acts 21:18-25, we read this.

> On the following day Paul went in with us to James, and all the elders were present. When he had greeted them, he

told in detail those things which God had done among
the Gentiles through his ministry. And when they heard
it, they glorified the Lord. And they said to him, "You
see, brother, how many myriads of Jews there are who
have believed, and they are all zealous for the law; but
they have been informed about you that you teach all the
Jews who are among the Gentiles to forsake Moses, saying that they ought not to circumcise their children nor to
walk according to the customs. What then? The assembly
must certainly meet, for they will hear that you have come.
Therefore do what we tell you: We have four men who
have taken a vow. Take them and be purified with them,
and pay their expenses so that they may shave their heads,
and that all may know that those things of which they
were informed concerning you are nothing, but that you
yourself also walk orderly and keep the law. But concerning the Gentiles who believe, we have written and decided
that they should observe no such thing, except that they
should keep themselves from things offered to idols, from
blood, from things strangled, and from sexual immorality."

When Paul arrived in Jerusalem, he was received warmly.
Before James and all the elders, Paul gave a detailed account
of the things that were being done through his ministry among
the Gentiles. The result was that these Jewish saints in Jerusalem greatly glorified God. But a problem had preceded him.
A false report concerning Paul and his teaching had arrived in
the Jerusalem church before Paul had. *This report was that he
taught Jewish Christians to cease circumcising their infant sons.* As the
context clearly shows, it was a *false* report. James knew it to
be false and suggested a plan whereby Paul could clear himself, demonstrating to the saints in Jerusalem that he himself
"walked orderly." Paul had undertaken a Nazarite vow, and
he was asked to pay the expenses of four of the saints in
Jerusalem who had done the same. In the course of discharg-

ing his obligations that were associated with this vow, Paul was attacked at the Temple by those outside the Christian faith—this time with the intent to take his life.

Now this whole incident could be interpreted as a regrettable lapse of consistency on Paul's part. In other words, one could argue that the slander attributed to Paul was not really a slander at all, and that Paul really *did* teach the Christian Jews to abandon circumcising their sons. Further, he should never have tried to obscure this fact through participation in the Nazarite vows of others. The line of reasoning is that Paul just did not stand up to James at this point. But of course, this "vacillating Paul" is not the Paul of the New Testament—especially on *this* kind of issue. Paul was the one who took on Peter at Antioch. Paul was the one who adamantly refused to circumcise Titus. Paul is the one who extended the right hand of fellowship to James, while at the same time asserting that they all were under the authority of the gospel, not over it. The truth of the gospel, he maintained, did not depend upon those who are "reputed to be pillars."

Further, this is not at all how Paul understood his actions in this situation. Notice what he says just a chapter later, still in chains as a result of his supposed "compromise." "Then Paul, looking earnestly at the council, said, 'Men and brethren, I have lived in all good conscience before God until this day'" (Acts 23:1). Paul does not have the attitude here of a man who has compromised on one of the essentials of the faith, and has gotten into deep trouble as a result. He knows, and testifies, that his conscience is clear.

An additional problem with the view that this was an unrighteous compromise is the unbiblical light in which it puts James. James was also an apostle, brother of the Lord, and an author of a portion of the New Testament. If Paul were compromised here (the thinking goes), the compromise was just a temporary and regrettable lapse. But what shall we say about James, who applied all the pressure to get Paul to this point of compromise? What shall we say about the elders of the Jerusalem church, with whom Paul was eager to maintain fellowship throughout the course of his ministry? It is true that certain men associated with James did not have a good grasp of the liberty of the New Covenant (Gal. 2:12), but it is equally clear that James, along with the whole church, repudiated them (Acts 15:24). The conclusion seems clear. Neither James nor Paul compromised the gospel in any way. To insist that they were sinning in this situation has no real grounds in the text.

This brings us to the meaning of Christian circumcision. Now if James and Paul did not compromise the gospel, then what happened in Acts 21? We must recall that circumcision was not a cultural badge; *properly understood*, it was the sign of the covenant promise made with Abraham. In other words, *it was a covenantal act*. When we are considering how circumcision was practiced by Abraham, Isaac and Jacob in the Old Testament, this point is granted by all. In its institution, circumcision was certainly covenantal, and in its *faithful* practice it remained that way.

Circumcision A.D.

But how was circumcision understood in the 1st century *after Christ*? It was certainly fading away, but how was it understood by *Christians* in the meantime? Consider what we know from the New Testament about the practice of covenantal circumcision within the Christian church of the first century.

First, circumcision remained an ordinance of God, marking the initiation of the one who received it as a member of the visible covenant community. Circumcision continued to mean that the one who received it was under an obligation to be a true son of Abraham—i.e. a *Christian*. There is no hint in the New Testament that circumcision ceased having a religious signification; there is a tremendous amount of teaching concerning the true *Christian* signification of it. For just one example, circumcision (as practiced by Christian Jews) pictured the removal of the body of sins of the flesh (Col. 2:11).

Second, the fact that many unbelieving Jews who opposed the gospel of Christ had been physically circumcised was considered by the Christians to be an apostate abuse of circumcision. The continued practice of such unbelieving circumcision was really Satan worship (Rev. 3:9), by people who *falsely claimed* to be true Jews. The problem with these unbelievers was not that their flesh was circumcised; the problem was that their hearts were *not* circumcised. Christians, both Jew and Gentile, were the *true* circumcision (Phil. 3:3). But the practice of unbelieving circumcision was not viewed as a neutral and cultural ethnic emblem; it was seen by Christians as a sacramental rebellion against God. To whom much is given, much is required. The practice of unbelieving circumcision put the Jews *first in line* to receive the judgment of God: "but to those who are self-seeking and do not obey the truth, but obey unrighteousness—indignation and wrath, tribulation and anguish, on every soul of man who does evil, of the Jew first and also of the Greek" (Rom. 2:8-9).

In the third place, circumcision of infants continued to be standard practice among Jewish Christians. The advent of Christ did not result in Jewish parents starting to wait until their children made a profession of faith before they were circumcised. The Jewish Christians did not suddenly switch to "believer's circumcision." Infant sons of Jewish Christians continued to be circumcised on the eighth day after birth.

Fourth, circumcision for adults, who sought in some significant sense to be identified with the Jews, continued to be practiced. The example here is Timothy, who had a Jewish mother and Greek father. Apparently Timothy sought to live culturally as a Jewish Christian ministering to unbelieving Jews, but because he was uncircumcised this was offensive to the Jews. Paul therefore was willing to circumcise him. "Paul wanted to have him go on with him. And he took him and circumcised him because of the Jews who were in that region, for they all knew that his father was Greek" (Acts 16:3).

But fifth, circumcision of Gentiles as a spiritual *requirement* was fiercely opposed by those who understood the gospel of grace (Acts 15). When some false brethren tried to insist on the circumcision of Titus, a Gentile, Paul fought the suggestion on the grounds that the gospel itself was at stake (Gal. 2:3-5). A Gentile who allowed himself to be circumcised, on the conditions of legalistic false teachers, had fallen from grace (Gal. 5: 3-4). Paul considered this to be of the utmost importance.

Sixth, although they were entangled in soul-destroying error, a significant faction within the professing Christian church did *not* believe the apostolic teaching that it was acceptable to receive the Gentiles on the grounds of their baptism alone (Acts 11:2-3; 15: 5). They were called Judaizers, and maintained that Gentiles had to be circumcised if they wanted to be saved. "And certain men came down from Judea and taught the brethren, 'Unless you are circumcised according to the custom of Moses, you cannot be saved'" (Acts 15:1).

Finally, another group existed within the church, apparently more teachable than the Judaizers, but not as mature in their covenantal understanding as Peter or Paul. When Peter was preaching to Gentiles at the house of Cornelius, and the Holy Spirit was given to them, note the response of a group there called the "circumcision who believed." "And those of the circumcision who believed were astonished, as many as came with Peter, because the gift of the Holy Spirit had been poured out on the Gentiles also" (Acts 10:45). Peter's response is also very significant. In the presence of "the circumcision who believed," he cites the giving of the Spirit as the reason for commanding that these Gentiles *be baptized*.

The "circumcision" was not a term that included all Christian Jews—Peter and Paul obviously did not belong to their number, although they were both circumcised Jews and had both believed. But neither were the "circumcision" to be completely identified with the *false* brethren of the Judaizing party. Notice how Paul speaks affectionately of some of them in the book of Colossians. "Aristarchus my fellow prisoner greets you, with Mark the cousin of Barnabas (about whom you received instructions: if he comes to you, welcome him), and Jesus who is called Justus. These are my only fellow workers for the kingdom of God who are of the circumcision; they have proved to be a comfort to me" (Col. 4:10-11).

New Spiritual Emblem

It cannot be emphasized too strongly that circumcision for Jewish Christians had a deep covenantal significance. This was of course true of those professing Christians for whom it had an erroneous significance (the Judaizers). But it was also covenantally and religiously important for the Jews who were *not* Judaizers. So intense was their feeling about it that they had to be *persuaded* to accept uncircumcised Gentiles into the church at all. But because of the faithfulness of men like Peter and Paul at the Jerusalem council, the Christian church (still overwhelmingly Jewish) began to accept uncircumcised Gentiles into their midst. These Gentiles were accepted into the visible church of the New Israel on the grounds of their *baptism*—a water baptism which could not be denied them because God had clearly baptized them with the Holy Spirit. Paul insisted on this truth with the Galatians, who were being troubled by some Jews for whom this water baptism was insufficient.

> For you are all sons of God through faith in Christ Jesus.
> For as many of you as were baptized into Christ have put
> on Christ. There is neither Jew nor Greek, there is neither
> slave nor free, there is neither male nor female; for you are
> all one in Christ Jesus. And if you are Christ's, then you
> are Abraham's seed, and heirs according to the promise
> (Gal. 3:26-29).

These Gentiles were sons of God through faith in Christ. Anyone who was *baptized* into Christ had put on Christ. Because of this, there was no longer a meaningful religious distinction between ethnic Jew and ethnic Greek. If someone is baptized into Christ, he belongs to Christ. If he belongs to Christ, a former stone-worshiping pagan is now a son of *Abraham*, and an heir according to the promise given to *Abraham*—whether or not he was circumcised. His baptism was covenantally sufficient. As Paul states here, water baptism included the Gentiles in the visible community of the New Israel, created by the New Covenant with Israel and the house of Judah.

Water baptism was also the emblem of the Spirit's work in joining the faithful Jews—the faithful remnant of Old Israel—to believing Gentiles in the commonwealth of New Israel, creating one new man out of the two. Now the Bible tells us that believing Jews continued to circumcise their sons, while graciously not insisting that the Gentiles start circumcising *their sons*. The debate in the early church was not whether the Jews should *stop* circumcising their sons; it was whether the Gentiles had to *start*. The decision of the Jerusalem council was *not* that individual Gentiles did not have to be circumcised. If circumcision had been required of them, it would have obligated them to live as Jews under the Mosaic law—which included the circumcision *of all subsequent generations*. Circumcision was not being waived for individual Gentiles; circumcision was being waived for Gentiles *and their seed*. So the

Christian church did not insist that Gentiles circumcise their infants—not because they were infants, but because they were *Gentile* infants.

Again, it is important to remember that we know Jewish continuance in circumcising their sons met with the approval of James, the elders at Jerusalem, and also *Paul*. Paul himself "walked orderly." If he had gotten married as a Christian, and if he had had a son, *he would have circumcised him.*

Christian Synagogue

The next thing we must consider is the existence of Christian *synagogues*, and the relationship of circumcision to membership in that synagogue. In the book of James, we are given very clear teaching on how we must avoid partiality in our treatment of individuals who come to worship with us. James says this:

> For if there should come into your assembly a man with gold rings, in fine apparel, and there should also come in a poor man in filthy clothes, and you pay attention to the one wearing the fine clothes and say to him, "You sit here in a good place," and say to the poor man, "You stand there," or, "Sit here at my footstool," have you not shown partiality among yourselves, and become judges with evil thoughts? (James 2:2-4)

The point here is not to rehearse James's point about partiality—although of course such warnings are never out of date. The point to be made is from James' use of two words. The word translated "assembly" is literally *synagogue*. Another word to note is *your*—he says *your* synagogue, implying that there is a plurality of synagogues. This quite consistent with what we saw earlier in James's comment to Paul in Acts 21. "Myriads" of Jews had believed. There had been three thousand on the first day alone, so obviously there had to be numerous meeting places for them. James refers to these assemblies of Christian Jews as *synagogues*. These same Christian Jews, as we have established, continued to circumcise their sons, and were organized in a network of believing synagogues. It is significant that these synagogues are described later in the book of James as *churches* (5:14).

This presents an obvious question. What was the relationship between circumcision and membership in the synagogue? Suppose a Jewish Christian father has just circumcised his son. Would that son have the same relation to the Christian synagogue of his father that a child of a modern baptist has to his father's church? Were such circumcised boys *members* of the Christian covenant community or not? How would the Jewish parents, under the instruction of the apostles, have understood their child's relationship to their synagogue?

In asking this question, we must remember that *synagogue* and *church* are two terms which are referring to the same thing. An American *church* and a Scottish *kirk* are the same thing—a local assembly of saints. The difference in the word does not matter. In the same way a Gentile Christian *ecclesia* and a Jewish Christian *synagogue* were the same thing—a visible, local gathering of saints. So what relationship would a small Jewish boy (three weeks old) have with the synagogue of his father?

Let us put this question another way. In the New Testament, were *any* infants legitimate members of *any* visible Christian covenant community? If we say *no*, then we are saying one of two things. Either the apostles were wrong to permit this practice which the New Testament records—they should have insisted that Christian Jews cease circumcising their boys— or the apostles changed the signification of circumcision in Christian homes so that it was merely a neutral cultural thing— "Jews had circumcision and Romans had togas."

The problem with the first option is that it undercuts and destroys apostolic authority. When Peter wavered at Antioch, the apostolic record does not leave us wondering on the point. We know that he was wrong in his hypocrisy and that Paul consequently opposed him to his face. But to charge the apostles with error on this issue is to say that their example *and* teaching were unreliable. If that is the case, then let us eat, drink, and be merry, for tomorrow we die. The second option is no better. The writers of the New Testament *always* treated circumcision as a God-ordained rite with tremendous covenantal significance—either for blessings or cursings. The New Testament contains no indication that the apostles downgraded circumcision from covenantal status to a mere ethnic emblem. On the contrary, they vigorously attacked circumcision among the unbelieving Jews because a holy thing was being profaned by disobedience and unbelief. They also attacked the attempt to circumcise Gentiles on the ground that *baptism* was revealed by Christ as sufficient for Gentiles. The Lord had commanded that the Gentiles be brought into discipleship through baptism. Jesus said to disciple the nations, *baptizing* them—He did not say to circumcise them.

This leaves us with the third option. Circumcision of an infant meant that the infant was, as a result, a member of the local synagogue. So if there was Christian circumcision (and there was), and if there were Christian synagogues (and there were), and if the Christians who went to these synagogues were the same believers who circumcised their sons (and they were), then the necessary conclusion is that *we know with certainty* that some first century Christian churches had infant members.

So believing Jews continued to practice circumcision, which placed their sons into membership in a visible assembly of Christian saints—the Christian synagogue. But the Jews were *also* to be baptized. We know this because the New Israel, Jew and Gentile alike, had one Lord, one faith, one *baptism* (Eph. 4:5). When Peter preached to the *Jews* on the day of

Pentecost, he told them that they needed to repent and be *baptized*, because the promise was for them and their *children* (Acts 2:39).

So the believing Gentiles had baptism, while the believing Jews had circumcision *and* baptism. Circumcision was retained by the Jews, prohibited to the Gentiles as a spiritual requirement, and baptism was commanded of them both. Incidentally, we can see clearly in retrospect that baptism, being required of both Jew and Gentile, was intended by Christ to be the lasting sign of initiation into the church. Under the providence of God and the teaching and leadership of the apostles, circumcision was "fading away," along with the rest of the *cultus* of the Old Covenant. The decisive point in this was the destruction of Jerusalem in 70 A.D., and the subsequent transformation of the church into a largely Gentile assembly. But *while* circumcision was fading away, it continued to be practiced by thousands in a way that affected the membership of the visible church of the first century. The apostles approved and taught this practice, and we have seen that they were right in doing so. This means we can say with confidence that the first century Christian church legitimately had at least *some* infant members—circumcised sons of believing Jews.

A Great Transition

We commonly assume that the formation of the Christian church in the first century was an abrupt lurch into a completely different order of things. In reality, the transition from the older administration to the new took *almost half a century*. Pentecost occurred around 30 A.D., and the formal judicial dissolution of the older Judaic worship occurred in 70 A.D. in the destruction of Jerusalem. Practically, what does this mean? It means that if a Jewish Christian couple had a boy within the first year after Pentecost, they easily could have seen the circumcision of their *great-grandson* before Jerusalem was destroyed. This period of time between Pentecost and the destruction of Jerusalem was the time when a great transition from circumcision to baptism was being accomplished. During this period, Gentiles were being included into fellowship with the believing Jews, but Jewish infants *were not being excluded.*

Those outside the Christian church were pagans and false Jews—Jews who apostatized from the covenant by rejecting Christ. We know that within the church were believing Gentiles and believing Jews, as well as the infants of believing Jews. The infants of believing Jews were given the sign of circumcision, which, even though it was an ordinance that was fading away, still had profound spiritual and covenantal significance.

This obviously brings us to the interesting and pertinent question of the *baptism* of Jewish infants. The first thing we must show is that circumcision and baptism have the same theological and doctrinal import. From what has been discussed above, this has already been established, but the point can be made even more strongly.

Baptism and Circumcision—A Comparison

Do circumcision and baptism refer to the same spiritual realities? If they do, and one is required for infants, then the other cannot be excluded *because of what it signifies.* If excluded at all, it would have to be excluded on other grounds. But the baptistic argument requires that it be excluded under the New Covenant *because of what it signifies.* Indeed, this insistence is the source of much of the initial plausibility of the baptist case. We think baptism signifies things that common sense tells us are not ordinarily seen in the experience of infants. But circumcision and baptism point away, not in. They point to the same Christ, and, in Scripture, this testimony of Christ was placed upon infants by Christian parents.

In Titus 3:5, baptism signifies regeneration—and Christ is our regeneration: "not by works of righteousness which we have done, but according to His mercy He saved us, through the washing of regeneration and renewing of the Holy Spirit." Baptism testifies to the washing and forgiveness which are the result of the Spirit's work in regeneration. But circumcision signifies regeneration as well. "For he is not a Jew who is one outwardly, nor is circumcision that which is outward in the flesh; but he is a Jew who is one inwardly; and circumcision is that of the heart, in the Spirit, not in the letter; whose praise is not from men but from God" (Rom. 2:28-29). In this passage, circumcision is a clear picture of the removal of our fleshly rebellion, which is the result of the Spirit's work in regeneration.

Baptism also signifies justification by faith—and Christ is our righteousness. The close association of faith (belief) and baptism is abundantly plain throughout the New Testament. "He who believes and is baptized will be saved; but he who does not believe will be condemned" (Mark 16:16). But circumcision points to justification by faith in another also. "And he received the sign of circumcision, a seal of the righteousness of the faith which he had while still uncircumcised, that he might be the father of all those who believe, though they are uncircumcised, that righteousness might be imputed to them also, and the father of circumcision to those who not only are of the circumcision, but who also walk in the steps of the faith which our father Abraham had while still uncircumcised" (Rom. 4:11-12).

Abraham was justified by faith before he was circumcised (*his* was a case of believer's circumcision). Because he was subsequently circumcised, he was therefore equipped to be the father of two groups of people—those who shared his faith without ever having been circumcised at all (Gentiles), and those who came to share his faith after their circumcision as infants (believing Jews). The fact that Abraham was justified by faith without circumcision meant that any man could be justified apart from circumcision. This was therefore an encouragement to Gentiles. The fact that Abraham was then given circumcision as a sign and seal of his faith-righteousness meant that this was its proper signification, and faithful Christian Jews were required to regard it as a sign, in their bodies, of the justification of Christ, appropriated by faith in the gospel.

Baptism also signifies the death and burial of the old man—and Christ is our death and burial. The young Christian has been crucified with Christ, and buried with Him in baptism. "Or do you not know that as many of us as were baptized into Christ Jesus were baptized into His death? Therefore we were buried with Him through baptism into death, that just as Christ was raised from the dead by the glory of the Father, even so we also should walk in newness of life. For if we have been united together in the likeness of His death, certainly we also shall be in the likeness of His resurrection, knowing this, that our old man was crucified with Him, that the body of sin might be done away with, that we should no longer be slaves of sin. For he who has died has been freed from sin" (Rom. 6:3-7). But this removal of the old man is also portrayed in circumcision. In baptism, the old man is portrayed as buried. In circumcision, the old man is pictured as surgically removed. "In Him you were also circumcised with the circumcision made without hands, by putting off the body of the sins of the flesh, by the circumcision of Christ" (Col. 2:11).

There are more parallels between baptism and circumcision. Baptism also signifies citizenship in the New Israel. The middle wall of partition has fallen, and Jews and Gentiles are brought together through "one Lord, one faith, one baptism"

(Eph. 4:5). Paul also teaches that those who are baptized are all one, regardless of race, gender, or class status. "For you are all sons of God through faith in Christ Jesus. For as many of you as were baptized into Christ have put on Christ. There is neither Jew nor Greek, there is neither slave nor free, there is neither male nor female; for you are all one in Christ Jesus. And if you are Christ's, then you are Abraham's seed, and heirs according to the promise" (Gal. 3:26-29). In short, baptism says that the baptized one is a true son of Abraham, and an heir of the promise given to him. He is a citizen of the true Israel. This is also what circumcision says. Circumcision signified citizenship in Israel. "And the uncircumcised male child, who is not circumcised in the flesh of his foreskin, that person shall be cut off from his people; he has broken My covenant" (Gen. 17:14).

Baptism is also to be taken very seriously. It brings with it a blessing on the obedient, and curses on the disobedient. Paul reminds the Corinthians that the fathers in the wilderness had all been baptized, and were communicants in the Rock of Christ.

> Moreover, brethren, I do not want you to be unaware that all our fathers were under the cloud, all passed through the sea, all were baptized into Moses in the cloud and in the sea, all ate the same spiritual food, and all drank the same spiritual drink. For they drank of that spiritual Rock that followed them, and that Rock was Christ. But with most of them God was not well pleased, for their bodies were scattered in the wilderness. Now these things became our examples, to the intent that we should not lust after evil things as they also lusted. And do not become idolaters as were some of them. As it is written, "The people sat down to eat and drink, and rose up to play." Nor let us commit sexual immorality, as some of them did, and in one day twenty-three thousand fell; nor let us tempt Christ, as some of them also tempted, and were

destroyed by serpents; nor complain, as some of them also complained, and were destroyed by the destroyer. Now all these things happened to them as examples, and they were written for our admonition, upon whom the ends of the ages have come. Therefore let him who thinks he stands take heed lest he fall (1 Cor. 10:1-12).

Paul expressly says that the Gentile Christians at Corinth were to take heed to this example. The fact that they had been baptized into Christ, and participated in the Lord's Supper, would not keep them from judgment. The history of the Jews' contempt for *their* wilderness baptism and table of communion was written as a warning and example to Christians. Blessings and curses are associated with our reception and treatment of the ordinances or sacraments given to us by God.

The same was of course true with circumcision. Signs given by God should not be the objects of our trifling. Circumcision also brought with it a blessing on the obedient, and curses on the disobedient. "For circumcision is indeed profitable if you keep the law; but if you are a breaker of the law, your circumcision has become uncircumcision" (Rom. 2:25). Because of the covenant represented in circumcision, the gospel was presented first to the Jew. If he rejected it (as many did), the judgment of God came first to the Jew.

Some Ramifications

When the foregoing is carefully considered, the ramifications become obvious. If a Jewish Christian couple presented a circumcised infant to the elders of the synagogue for baptism, on what grounds could they be denied? All the modern baptistic arguments fall flat. For example, if we say that baptism signifies a heart-felt appeal to God (1 Pet. 3:21), and that the child has not yet *personally* done this, the parents could respond that circumcision signifies heart religion as well (Rom. 2:28-29), but that it was fully proper to circumcise him. Circumcision represents true worship of God in the Spirit. "For we are the circumcision, who worship God in the Spirit, rejoice in Christ Jesus, and have no confidence in the flesh" (Phil. 3:3). True worship is seen in the sign of circumcision. But an infant is incapable of true worship (the argument goes). But this argument is not made with regard to *circumcision* in either the Old Covenant or the New. So why is it made with regard to baptism?

Some might argue that baptism would be excluded because it was superfluous. Why administer *both* baptism and circumcision to an infant? The answer of course is that during this time, God required both of all the Jews. Baptism was required to display the unity of believing Jews with believing Gentiles (Eph. 4:5), and circumcision was required to show the unity of believing Jews with Abraham (Rom. 4:11-12). The fact that believing Jews were both circumcised and baptized showed that Gentiles were also unified with Jews *as the true seed of Abraham.*

Obviously, this brings us next to the question of Gentile infants. Circumcision was prohibited for such—not because they were infants, but because they were Gentiles. So would the children of such believing Gentiles need to wait until they made a personal profession of faith, and *then* receive baptism? To do this would establish and maintain a practice that the New Testament very strongly prohibits—a sharp class division between Jews and Gentiles within the church. A situation would immediately develop where children of Jews would grow up as members of the church (because they had been circumcised and baptized), while the children of Gentiles were excluded (because they had not been baptized). This would maintain the Judaizing pressure on Gentile fathers to submit to circumcision—so that their sons could be circumcised too, in order to be included in the covenant. But this line of thought was not necessary because Gentiles were accepted on the strength of their baptism. So would baptism be offered to the children of Gentiles? *Of course.*

Jew and Gentile alike were required and expected to live in harmony within the church, all bearing the same mark or badge—that of *Christian.* The middle wall of partition had come down. But because circumcision was prohibited to Gentiles as Gentiles, circumcision could not be their common mark of unity. If Jews did not take the mark of baptism, then that could not be the sign of unity either. Therefore believing Jews were baptized. Confirming this line of reasoning is the fact that we have express statements of Scripture cited earlier recording how Jews received water baptism.

The Real Debate

In conclusion, the way baptists and paedobaptists handle the modern debate over infant baptism frequently shows how far removed we are from the debates of the first century. *Our* debates center around a question like this: "Do you mean to say that you think the Gentiles in the first century baptized their *infants*? Where do you get *that*?" In the first century the question was more like this: "Do you mean to say that the Gentiles don't have to *circumcise* their infants?" It was a foregone conclusion in the first century that *something* must be done with the infants—after all, if at least one parent was a believer, the children were *holy* (1 Cor. 7:14).

The modern debate over baptism has suffered because the close grammatical questions have far overshadowed the broader historical questions. It is too easy for the historical/grammatical approach to wind up being simply the grammatical approach alone. But if, for whatever reason, the historical context is neglected, this means the passage will be interpreted in the light of an implicit *modern* historical context. There is never "no context." This problem is illustrated whenever the question of infant baptism is addressed by someone who says there is no place in the New Testament which says, "And Paul baptized the infant Julius."

As we have made plain, this question of historical context is related directly to the question of infant baptism. If we examine the history of the Jews prior to Christ (for two millennia) and the history of the Church after Christ (for a millennium and a half), searching both uninspired and inspired histories, we find absolutely *no debate* on the propriety of including infants *as infants* as members of the people of God (Tertullian notwithstanding). This debate among evangelical believers surfaced for the first time in the historical record in 1522 A.D. It is clear the modern debate over baptism is not part of the historical context of the Bible's teaching on baptism. We have exported it to the past; it is a debate which is not native to that past. Another way of saying this is that we misunderstand the New Testament because we have imposed *our* debates and questions on it. Instead of this, we should be seeking to understand what questions and problems the apostles were addressing. When we do this, the fact that infant baptism is indeed fitting, and required, becomes immediately apparent.

7

The Olive Tree and Olive Shoots

An Organic Connection

The Bible teaches that the people of God are *organically connected* to one another. This organic connection can be the source of great blessings, or of real spiritual dismay, depending upon the condition of the church. We are members of one another, and when one part of the body suffers, the whole body suffers with it.

As we begin to discuss the nature of this organic connection, it is crucial to recognize from the outset that no true child of God can ever fall away from the faith in a final and complete way. It is important for us to remember that the elect are singled out in God's mind from before the foundation of the world, and they are singled out for glorification. Those whom He foreknew, He predestined, and those whom He predestined, He glorified.

Of course this doctrine of the saints' preservation and perseverance is precious to believers. But the doctrine does not teach it is impossible for a *professing* believer to fall away. Many have done so, and will continue to do so. We know from Scripture that when this happens it is a matter of an unregenerate person revealing his true condition. At the point of apostasy, it is clear that he was never a disciple indeed.

"Then Jesus said to those Jews who believed Him, 'If you abide in My word, you are My disciples indeed'" (John 8:31). There is a distinction made here between a disciple, and a disciple *indeed*. Christ is speaking generally to Jews who had *believed* in Him, and goes on to show that it is possible that some of them had not *really* believed. The Bible teaches that the apostasy of the elect is an impossibility (God cannot lie), but it also teaches that apostasy is a very real sin. But if it is not a hypothetical sin, then who commits it? The answer is professing Christians who are lying to themselves and others about their true spiritual condition.

Covenantal Apostates

The apostle John speaks of some false teachers in a way that reveals this truth. "They went out from us, but they were not of us; for if they had been of us, they would have continued with us; but they went out that they might be made manifest, that none of them were of us" (1 John 2:19). But is such a person a disciple *at all*? The biblical answer is that they certainly are. The fact that someone professes covenantal allegiance hypocritically does not alter the objective facts concerning what he has said and done. A man may lie at the altar about his intention to be faithful to his bride. But his hypocrisy does not keep him from entering into the married state. An oath, when taken, *binds*. When it is a lying oath, then the sin is truly grievous precisely because the oath binds.

A man who rejects the gospel from within the covenant is in far worse position than a man who has never heard the gospel at all. To whom much is given, much is required. "Of how much worse punishment, do you suppose, will he be thought worthy who has trampled the Son of God underfoot, counted the blood of the covenant by which he was sanctified a common thing, and insulted the Spirit of grace?" (Heb. 10:29) The man caught up in this horrible sin of apostasy was treating the blood of Christ as a common thing. But it was not just the blood of Christ considered in the abstract, it was the blood by which this particular covenant-breaker was *sanctified*. This covenant-breaker had a certain kind of covenantal holiness which was defiled by his personal unholiness. The inevitable result of this kind of hypocrisy is a "worse punishment" than was ever received under the administration of the Levitical ordinances.

New Covenant Curses

There is a very common assumption among modern Christians that the blessings associated with the New Covenant are tremendous. This is of course accurate, but along with this assumption comes the unbiblical idea that the curses for despising and abusing the New Covenant are nil. This is false. The Bible teaches that there is a correspondence between the greatness of our salvation and the greatness of the covenantal condemnation for those who abuse that salvation through their apostasy. "For if the word spoken through angels proved steadfast, and every transgression and disobedience received a just reward, how shall we escape if we neglect so great a salvation, which at the first began to be spoken by the Lord, and was confirmed to us by those who heard Him" (Heb. 2:2-3). In other words, if one thinks that justice was swift and severe for those who despised the Levitical administration, *how much more* should he guard against abusing the New Covenant. The author of Hebrews is just simply appalled at the thought of what happens to those who neglect such a great salvation.

But how can this be? Why is it any worse for unbelievers who fall from the covenant than for unbelievers who never had a relationship to the covenant? The answer has to do with the position they have in Christ, and against which they rebel through fruitlessness.

> I am the true vine, and My Father is the vinedresser. Every
> branch in Me that does not bear fruit He takes away; and
> every branch that bears fruit He prunes, that it may bear
> more fruit. You are already clean because of the word which
> I have spoken to you. Abide in Me, and I in you. As the
> branch cannot bear fruit of itself, unless it abides in the
> vine, neither can you, unless you abide in Me. I am the
> vine, you are the branches. He who abides in Me, and I in
> him, bears much fruit; for without Me you can do noth-
> ing. If anyone does not abide in Me, he is cast out as a
> branch and is withered; and they gather them and throw
> them into the fire, and they are burned (John 15:1-6).

For many Christians, this is a "problem passage." We
want Christ to use a different figure. We want Him to be the
Marble Box, with us as the individual marbles. When we are
saved, we are put into the Marble Box, and we had better
watch it, or we might find ourselves taken out of the Marble
Box, losing our salvation. Or, if we know that salvation is not
a possession of *ours*, which we could lose, we want the Marble
Box to have a great big lock on it, and to be full of elect, non-
loseable marbles.

Now election is a thoroughly biblical doctrine. We are
Christ's possession, and He will not lose us. This is entirely a
scriptural sentiment, and true saints are directly encouraged
by Scripture to comfort themselves this way. "What then shall
we say to these things? If God is for us, who can be against
us? He who did not spare His own Son, but delivered Him
up for us all, how shall He not with Him also freely give us all
things? Who shall bring a charge against God's elect? It is God
who justifies" (Rom. 8:31-33).

But this consolation nevertheless leaves us with a problem. If one of God's elect cannot lose his salvation, and cannot be removed from the vine, then who *is* removed from
the vine? Christians who hold that it is possible for a true

Christian to lose his salvation can easily use this passage to show that it is possible to be removed from the Vine. But they then have an impossible time with the teaching of Scripture elsewhere on the unchangeable nature of God's purposes in the salvation of His elect.

On the other hand, baptistic Christians who hold that salvation cannot be lost do not have a problem with the promises connected to election, but they do have a monumental problem *here*, in this passage. In order to be removed from the Vine, someone must have really been attached to the Vine. Christ is not issuing idle threats. Still less is He terrifying His saints with hypothetical possibilities which are actually impossibilities. Now of course, true saints will regularly examine their own hearts in the light of such warnings, but the warnings are not directly addressed to them. So what is Christ talking about then?

Dead Branch Removal

There really are people who really are removed from the Vine. They are described in Scripture as *branches which bear no fruit*. The Bible teaches that these are people who are connected to Christ (they have to be connected to Him in order to be removed from him), who nevertheless have no saving interest in Him. If they were regenerate, they would bear fruit. They are not regenerate, but they *are* attached to the Vine. And in God's providence, the fruitless branches are removed.

It is important for us to remember that Christ has already spoken in the gospel of John concerning the importance of abiding in Him. We earlier addressed the distinction Christ made between his nominal followers and His disciples *indeed*. That passage bears closer examination.

> Then Jesus said to those Jews who believed Him, "If you abide in My word, you are My disciples indeed. And you

shall know the truth, and the truth shall make you free."
They answered Him, "We are Abraham's descendants,
and have never been in bondage to anyone. How can you
say, 'You will be made free'?" Jesus answered them, "Most
assuredly, I say to you, whoever commits sin is a slave of
sin. And a slave does not abide in the house forever, but
a son abides forever (John 8:31-35).

A disciple indeed is someone who is set free. Such freedom is the result of abiding in Christ's Word, knowing the
Truth, and being set free by the Truth. These Jews who had
professed belief in Christ, however, bridled at this promise.
How could they be *set* free when they already *were* free? Their
covenantal presumption comes right to the surface—after all,
they were Abraham's descendants. Jesus answers them by saying that whoever commits sin is a *slave* to sin. In addition, He
continues His doctrine and reveals something important about
the nature of *abiding*. In this passage, Christ is using the figure
of a house. Both sons and slaves abide in a house. What is the
difference between them? A slave does not abide in the house
forever, but a son does. In other words, while a slave may
make the house his temporary abode, he will be removed
from it. He is not an heir, and will not be counted among the
heirs. If the slave is confused, he may think himself a son, but
a day will come when his presumption is exposed for what it
is. As Christ teaches us the nature of abiding, we see that He is
not contrasting *abiding* with *not abiding*. The contrast is rather
between *abiding temporarily* and *abiding permanently*. In this fallen
world, apostasy, church discipline, fruitlessness, rebuke, and
scandal are to be expected. The house of Christ still has slaves
and sons, and we should not be surprised when the differences between them become manifest.

Christ is the Tree of Israel. This organic image applied to
the people of God is used by Paul, and in a most revealing
way. Furthermore, the image he uses sheds special light on the

biblical doctrine and practice of infant baptism. The Jews were the Israel of God. An image used of this Israel in Scripture is that of an olive tree. For good and evil, the house of Israel was an olive tree planted by the Lord (Jer. 11:16; Hos. 14:6). Anyone who was circumcised, or represented by one circumcised, had a place on this tree.

When the time had come for the salvation of the nations to be revealed, God did not chop down His olive tree in order to plant another one. It is true that the tree was overgrown and largely fruitless, but it was still redeemable by the Master Gardener. A significant minority of the branches were still good (Zech. 13:9). This is how He described His work through the apostle Paul.

> For if the firstfruit is holy, the lump is also holy; and if the root is holy, so are the branches. And if some of the branches were broken off, and you, being a wild olive tree, were grafted in among them, and with them became a partaker of the root and fatness of the olive tree, do not boast against the branches. But if you do boast, remember that you do not support the root, but the root supports you. You will say then, "Branches were broken off that I might be grafted in." Well said. Because of unbelief they were broken off, and you stand by faith. Do not be haughty, but fear. For if God did not spare the natural branches, He may not spare you either. Therefore consider the goodness and severity of God: on those who fell, severity; but toward you, goodness, if you continue in His goodness. Otherwise you also will be cut off. And they also, if they do not continue in unbelief, will be grafted in, for God is able to graft them in again. For if you were cut out of the olive tree which is wild by nature, and were grafted contrary to nature into a cultivated olive tree, how much more will these, who are natural branches, be grafted into their own olive tree? (Rom. 11:16-24).

The apostate Jews were broken off because of the fruit-lessness of their unbelief. They had no faith, and so they were removed from the tree. As Paul would say, this is said well enough. But how did they come to be attached to the tree in the first place? This olive tree was the Israel of God—how could any unbeliever be connected to such a tree? The answer is simple. There are only two ways to come into a connection with the tree—to grow on the tree as the vast majority of the Jews did, or be grafted on the tree as the first century Gentiles were. With the exception of proselytes to Judaism, the children of the covenant *grew on the tree*. But even though they were native to the olive tree, and had a natural connection to the root, they nevertheless produced *no olives*. Their problem was unbelief. But this lack of true faith, this lack of fruit, did not distress them. Hardened in their unbelief, they thought their position on the tree was automatically secure. It was not. John the Baptist had solemnly warned against this kind of covenantal blindness and folly. "And even now the ax is laid to the root of the trees. Therefore every tree which does not bear good fruit is cut down and thrown into the fire" (Matt. 3:10; Luke 3:9).

The Root of the Matter

Paul says here that the nature of the tree is determined by the nature of the root. A tree is not supported by her outer-most branches, just recently grafted in. Paul has to remind the Gentiles that the tree is not upside down. The branches are supported by the root; not the other way around. And what is this root? "And in that day there shall be a Root of Jesse, Who shall stand as a banner to the people; for the Gentiles shall seek Him, and His resting place shall be glorious" (Is. 11:10). Christ was the Root which supported the tree. He did not need the Jews, the Jews needed Him. He did not need the Gentiles, the Gentiles needed Him. If the root is removed from a tree, the tree will die. But the removal of branches is a common way to *save* a tree. Sinful men need to be warned about such things, both Jew and Gentile. But God knows the nature of the tree. His purpose is set, and He will bring forth abundant fruit. "Those who come He shall cause to take root in Jacob; Israel shall blossom and bud, and fill the face of the world with fruit" (Is. 27:6).

We see that Scripture never tolerates fruitlessness among those who have a connection with the tree. At the same time, we see that Scripture never encourages us to think of the tree in a Utopian fashion. It is a fact of history that the tree has had fruitless branches, and at certain times, *many* fruitless branches. But to encourage us, the Bible gives us a marked contrast between the tree we now see, which has both fruitful and fruitless branches, and the eschatological tree, which will fill the earth with fruit.

As far as the Jews were concerned, the Bible teaches that because they were born into an Israelite family, circumcised in the covenant on the eighth day, they were attached to the tree. This attachment was an objective historical fact. But the sin and hypocrisy of many of them was *also* an objective fact, and the Lord of the Orchard consequently removed their branches, and grafted in other branches. Now the interesting thing here is that Paul turns and warns the Gentiles who had been grafted in against *the very same sin* committed by their fruitless predecessors. But could not these Gentiles answer Paul in this fashion? "Paul, you misunderstand the nature of the New Covenant. In the New Covenant, *all* branches always bear fruit. The prophet Jeremiah promised that we would all know the Lord from the least of us to the greatest. Your warning is unnecessary."

Such a response is obviously wrong-headed. But what then, are we to make of Paul's warning? This passage is just a few pages after Paul's wonderful exultation in the fact that nothing can remove us from the love of God which is in Christ Jesus. So what is he talking about *here*? Why does Paul argue that nothing can remove the elect from Christ, and then turn around and deliver a sober warning about the dangers of being removed from the olive tree? The answer is inescapable. There is a difference between being *elect*, and being a *covenant member*. The elect cannot be removed from God's sovereign decree; professing Christians *can* be removed from among God's people, and they frequently are. When they are removed, their unregenerate status is revealed. They are not regenerate, and never were. But they were really in the covenant, a fact that now applies to them to their sorrow.

Paul is arguing that the nature of the tree has not been changed by the transition from the Levitical administration to the New Covenant. The Root is still Christ. The tree is still Israel—not the nation of Israel, but rather the person of Israel, the Lord Jesus. Christ is our Israel, *and Christ is our only Israel*. If we abide in Him permanently, we will bear fruit that remains. If we do not abide in Him permanently, we will be removed and burned.

The methods of the Master Gardener have not changed. Fruitless branches were removed in the First Reformation, when the unbelieving Jews were taken out of the Israel of God. Jesus clearly warned the unbelieving Jews. "Therefore I say to you, the kingdom of God will be taken from you and given to a nation bearing the fruits of it" (Matt. 21:43). The same thing happened again in the Second Reformation, fifteen hundred years later. The Gentiles who had been grafted in had forgotten Paul's warning to them. They thought their hereditary position in the tree was sufficient to keep them in the tree. "Are we not Christians?" was said with the same complacency and evil heart that "Are we not Jews?" had been said, equally in vain, hundreds of years before. God is not mocked. The outermost branches do not support the root.

We have seen that the children of Jews grew on the tree. For the unbelievers among them, their fleshly descent from Abraham was their point of pride and stumbling. It is crucial to realize that Paul does not dispute their presence on the tree at one time; he simply points out that there was no eternal security for covenant members. Not all Israel are Israel.

The question remains of the faithful Jewish branches who were not removed from the tree. They came to the tree the same way (they grew on it), but they remained on the tree because of their *faith*. But what of their children, the children of believing Jews in the first century? God's word is always constant. "Your wife shall be like a fruitful vine. In the very heart of your house, your children like olive plants all around your table. Behold, thus shall the man be blessed who fears the Lord. The Lord bless you out of Zion, and may you see the good of Jerusalem all the days of your life. Yes, may you see your children's children. Peace be upon Israel!" (Psalm 128:3-6). For those faithful Jews who remained on the olive tree, their children remained olive shoots.

Paul does not turn to these faithful Jews and say anything about a drastic change in the nature of the tree. He is explicit that there was a change in the bringing in of Gentile branches. This was done, not through circumcision, but rather through baptism (an interesting new grafting technique, which, for the Jews, took some getting used to). But Paul was also very plain about the necessity of the Gentiles guarding themselves against the same covenantal presumption that was the failing of the many branches on the ground.

Master Gardener at Work

Faith is the only way to maintain connection with the tree. But Paul is not teaching that only believers have a connection to the tree. This tree in Romans 11 is not a mystical tree in heaven, with no turmoil and disruption. It is the tree of God's covenant people, *planted in history*, and subject to periods of great growth and blessing, and subject to times of great disobedience and distress. But the Master Gardener knows His craft. He has promised that this tree will bear fruit, and the fruit of it will fill the earth. He knows what He is doing.

Because it is the tree of God's people in *history*, the tree has unregenerate branches. Some of the branches do not bear fruit. How does this come about in the Christian era? Paul's warning shows that it is the same tree, and the Gentiles will come to experience the same temptation which overwhelmed the Jews. Consequently, this temptation arises in the Christian aeon in the same way that it arose in the Levitical aeon. *Children of believing parents grow on the tree.* This is what happened with the Jews, this is where they stumbled, and this is what Paul warns the Gentiles not to repeat. Such children grow up, and soon there are children and grandchildren who are as nominal as their ancestors. When the church is faithful, gross forms of such nominalism are addressed through church discipline. But if it is not addressed, in time the tree will start to be overgrown. And when the tree gets in such a state, the temptation of the few remaining fruitful branches is to lament, and question God. "Why is this happening? Does the Lord not see?" But the Lord does see, and He has promised to maintain the tree.

Nominalism

If the nominal children of believers do not bear fruit, they will be removed. When they are removed, they are not being removed from the number of the elect, for they were never in that number. The elect cannot have their names erased from God's saving decree. Nevertheless, in a very real sense, these covenantal unbelievers are still removed from *something*. What are they removed from? The answer is that they are removed from among the covenant people. They have de-

spised the blood of the covenant, by which they were sanctified. So the fact that an unbeliever grew on the tree is no
source of blessing to him *at all*. The more nourishment he
derives from the tree, and the bigger he gets without any fruit,
the more there is to burn. There have been countless thousands who have had cause to curse the day they were born
into a covenant home; because of their unbelief, it only in-
creased their condemnation.

All Christians who love this tree of Christ hate to see it
overgrown with the wickedness of hypocrisy and nominalism. It is a natural reaction, therefore, to attempt to ensure
that all the branches bear fruit. This is good—we are commanded in the Bible to labor toward this end—but we must
be careful to do it the way the Bible says. In a zeal to get rid
of the tares, we must beware of a disobedient pulling up of
wheat. As we fight with the wolves we must not wound the
sheep.

In this image of the olive tree, Paul is *not* teaching us that
there is a fundamental difference between Jewish membership in the tree and Gentile membership in the tree. Rather,
his point is that there is a marked similarity—so much so that
he must give a very pointed warning to the Gentiles and their
offspring. This warning, as church history has demonstrated
time and again, was very much needed. It is not enough to be
"born" on the tree. A man must be born again—*he must bear
fruit.*

This means the baptists do have a point. Earlier in the
book of Romans, Paul had addressed certain truths about
God's covenant and the sin of nominalism. He does two things
there, both of which have application to the whole controversy between believers over infant baptism.

In the first place, Paul acknowledges that nominalism is a
genuine evil, and that it causes those outside the covenant to
revile and despise it.

> You who make your boast in the law, do you dishonor
> God through breaking the law? For 'the name of God is
> blasphemed among the Gentiles because of you,' as it is
> written. For circumcision is indeed profitable if you keep
> the law; but if you are a breaker of the law, your circumci-
> sion has become uncircumcision (Rom. 2:23-25).

What did the pagan Gentiles see when they looked at the
olive tree before the Lord pruned it? The second chapter of
Romans is a detailed catalog of the sins of the professed covenant people of God. In the first chapter, Paul had taken pains
to show that the Gentiles were condemned in their sin. But in
the second chapter he showed that the same problem of disobedience and sin afflicted the Jews as well. In the third chapter he demonstrated that Jew and Gentile alike were *both* under sin—"for all have sinned and fall short of the glory of
God" (Rom. 3:23).

In Rom. 2:23-25, Paul stated that as the Jews had lived in
a manner inconsistent with their law, the result was blasphemy
of the name of God on the part of Gentiles. Because the Jews
really were in covenant with God, their sin and disobedience
reflected on Him. If this was the case when rank infidels
mocked the God of the covenant, *how much more* does the
principle apply when fellow believers question our doctrine
and practice? The similarity is interesting. When a biblical
paedobaptist hears the charge of "nominalism" leveled against
the practice of baptizing infants, he ought not to take offense.
The response ought to be a humble grief. The charge is not
being manufactured from nothing. Why do baptists not understand the covenant? The answer is not what many paedobaptists want to hear—the baptists do not understand it
because *paedobaptists* do not understand it.

We should think for a moment. If there were a denomination of Christians which baptized their infants, and the parents reared all the children in the nurture and admonition of

the Lord, saw them overwhelmingly come to a faithful and consistent profession of faith, and then these children in turn brought up *their* children in the same way, and with the same success, we would all know the name of that denomination. Furthermore, every true Christian parent would want to be part of it. But there is currently no such group—although God has promised in the centuries to come *there will be*. We must continue to speak of the covenant because the Bible does, but until we live in our child-rearing as though we really believed in these covenantal blessings and promises, we must not be surprised that relatively few listen to what we say.

But Paul goes on. This admitted failure of the fruitless branches is not grounds for adopting a human solution to the problem. Far from reacting to this fruitlessness, Paul's response is to glory in the God who never changes. "What advantage then has the Jew, or what is the profit of circumcision? Much in every way! Chiefly because to them were committed the oracles of God. For what if some did not believe? Will their unbelief make the faithfulness of God without effect? Certainly not! Indeed, let God be true but every man a liar. As it is written: 'That You may be justified in Your words, and may overcome when You are judged'" (Rom. 3:1-4). Paul has already acknowledged that the sinfulness of the covenant people has resulted in blasphemy in the Gentile world. The Jews, the people of God, should therefore hang their heads in shame. But Paul does not permit us to draw any wrong conclusions about God from this. If the Jews at large did not bear fruit, Paul asks, what was the profit of circumcision? The answer is *much in every way*.

He asks the question, "What if some of the Jews did not believe?" His answer basically amounts to this—*So what?* We can point with amazement at the covenant people of God at the time of Christ. They murdered their own Messiah. Does this make God's faithfulness come to nothing? *Certainly not.*

Christendom has more than once been full of baptized infidels. Does this make God a liar? *Certainly not.* Paul then comes to a remarkable statement. Every last professing believer in the world could be lying, and doing so through the teeth, and God would still be true, the root would still be firm, the tree would still be Christ, and the earth will one day be full of fruit. God's promise to Abraham was not dependent upon the cooperation of man. And we are not supposed to believe it because we see it; we are to believe it because God says it.

All true Christians agree that fruitless branches on the tree of Christ are a scandal and an embarrassment. Their presence should grieve us, and we should employ every means sanctioned by Scripture to bring about their removal. As we seek to be faithful in such discipline, we realize that we do not have the ability to prune with the same intelligence shown by the Lord when He prunes. In fact, we have such little competence for such tasks (we cannot see the heart) that God commands us to limit ourselves to branches that are glaringly bad. We must guard against errors on both sides. There are some who are content to let the Lord do all the pruning, but they disobey His clear commands for church discipline. There are others who want to do all the pruning for Him, but they are equally in disobedience. We must never let our zeal for a pure and fruitful church take us beyond scriptural boundaries. We don't want to find ourselves in the curious position of requiring people to bear fruit *before* they are attached to the tree.

8

Father Abraham

The Father of Circumcision

A very important passage for understanding the whole question of circumcision and baptism is found in the fourth chapter of Romans. In that passage, Paul shows how Abraham is the father of *all* believers.

> Does this blessedness then come upon the circumcised only, or upon the uncircumcised also? For we say that faith was accounted to Abraham for righteousness. How then was it accounted? While he was circumcised, or uncircumcised? Not while circumcised, but while uncircumcised. And he received the sign of circumcision, a seal of the righteousness of the faith which he had while still uncircumcised, that he might be the father of all those who believe, though they are uncircumcised, that righteousness might be imputed to them also, and the father of circumcision to those who not only are of the circumcision, but who also walk in the steps of the faith which our father Abraham had while still uncircumcised (Rom. 4:9-12).

Paul is concerned to show that uncircumcised Gentiles can share the faith of Abraham, and be considered his legitimate spiritual descendants. He does this by pointing out that Abraham was put right with God *before* he was circumcised. This means he was a justified man, for a period of time, without having been circumcised. Consequently, he is a father to uncircumcised men who share his faith. He was justified without circumcision, therefore others may be justified without circumcision.

Now when Abraham was eventually circumcised, it was a sign and seal of the righteousness *he already had* by faith. That righteousness was Christ. But Paul then argues that Abraham's circumcision also made him the father of another group of individuals—circumcised Jews who also shared his faith. But there is a problem. What did Abraham have in common with these Jews? Of course it was faith, but it was also circumcision. But how did he have this in common with these Jews when his was a circumcision *after* justification, and theirs was a circumcision *before* justification? We should be able to see, therefore, that Abraham, who was circumcised after justification, is the father of all Jewish believers who were circumcised before justification. He was circumcised as an adult, and they were circumcised as infants—but for Paul's purpose here they were both just simply circumcised. Despite the difference between them with regard to the age when they were circumcised (adult/infant), and the difference between them concerning the circumcision's temporal placement with regard to justification (post/pre), Abraham is still called here the *father of circumcision.*

Three important truths emerge from this passage. Uncircumcised believing Abraham is thereby the father of uncircumcised believing Gentiles. Believing Abraham, circumcised after justification, is thereby the father of believing Jews, circumcised before justification. Abraham was circumcised as a sign and seal of the righteousness he had by faith. That righteousness was not his own personal faith, it was *Christ.* Circumcision was his seal that Christ, his righteousness, would in fact come. So when Abraham took this seal in his body, he was thus marked as the father of *all* believers in Christ—Jew and Gentile both. This is important to note because Abraham's circumcision was not his personal testimony of his own personal faith. It was God's testimony, sealing his righteousness—which must *not* be identified with his faith.

Timing Not Important

These truths demonstrate that the temporal placement of this sign of circumcision with regard to the time of justification was not significant in Paul's thinking. It is not central to his argument here in this passage. He does not say that Jews who come to faith must be circumcised again, in order to have a circumcision *like Abraham's*. If they have come to the faith of Abraham, then their circumcision, which they already had, is like Abraham's. If they did not come to the faith of Abraham, then their circumcision was just a mutilation of the flesh, and worse.

Thus if a Jew came to true saving faith (as Abraham did), then his pre-existent circumcision was evangelical. It was a gospel ordinance. Believing Jews did not have to get circumcised again in order for Abraham to be their father. The circumcision they had already received was sufficient. And if a Jew did not ever come to true saving faith, he was a son of the devil and not a son of Abraham—"Therefore know that only those who are of faith are sons of Abraham" (Gal. 3:7).

Incidentally, we must also remember the nature of circumcision. It was a mark that was borne permanently in the body. The issue was not so much whether someone *was* circumcised on such and such a date, but whether he *is* circumcised now. And, for Paul, if a man is circumcised now, then there had to be a correspondence between the mark he bore in his flesh and the circumcision of his heart. If there was not such a correspondence, the individual was under the judgment of God. In this passage Abraham is described as the father of believing Gentiles because he was justified while in an uncircumcised condition—being uncircumcised cannot be a barrier to justification. Abraham was a justified man in both conditions, circumcised and uncircumcised, and was therefore a father of faith to justified men in both conditions, circumcised and uncircumcised.

9

The Mode of Baptism

Contextual Considerations

In considering how baptism is to be administered, one basic question has to be asked and answered—how does the *Bible* use the word *baptism*? According to Scripture, what modes of baptism are used? And as our discussion proceeds it will be seen that the use of the plural *modes* above was not accidental.

Our first object should be to see how the words *baptize* and *baptism* are used in the Bible. We should look for our definitions of the word primarily in the *context* of its use in Scripture. There is a common temptation to set the definition of these words primarily on the basis of lexical reference and definition, rather than contextual study. And while *one* of the primary lexical definitions of the Greek word *baptizo* certainly is immersion, a contexual study will show that there are other uses as well. It should be noted as we proceed, however, that in what follows there is no dispute whatever about the propriety of immersion as a true form of Christian baptism. But as Scripture makes equally clear, we cannot limit ourselves to immersion only.

Pouring

First, in Acts 2, the word *baptism* refers to a pouring. We know that the experience at Pentecost was a *baptism* of the Holy Spirit because it is described as such, both before and after the event. Before He had ascended into heaven, Jesus told His disciples what would happen to them in the immediate future—they would be *baptized* with the Holy Spirit. He said, "For John truly baptized with water, but you shall be baptized with the Holy Spirit not many days from now" (Acts 1:5).

Later in the book of Acts, after he had been used by the Lord to bring the gospel to Cornelius and his household, Peter was called to give an account of his actions. He defended what had happened on the basis of the similarities between the giving of the Holy Spirit to the household of Cornelius and the giving of the Holy Spirit to Jewish disciples at Pentecost. 'Then I remembered the word of the Lord, how He said, 'John indeed baptized with water, but you shall be baptized with the Holy Spirit'" (Acts 11:16).

So, then, it should be very clear that the giving of the Holy Spirit at Pentecost is described as a *baptism*. But then Peter, immediately after the giving of the Spirit, when he comes to describe what has happened to the disciples, describes it as a fulfillment of prophecy from the prophet Joel: "And it shall come to pass in the last days, says God, That I will pour out of My Spirit on all flesh; your sons and your daughters shall prophesy, your young men shall see visions, your old men shall dream dreams" (Acts 2:17). And in the incident with the household of Cornelius, Peter's description of this baptism by the Holy Spirit is certainly not one of immersion, although fully consistent with a pouring. There the Holy Spirit is described by Peter as *falling* on Cornelius and those gathered with him. "And as I began to speak, the Holy Spirit fell upon them, as upon us at the beginning" (Acts 11:15).

God, in baptizing the disciples with the Holy Spirit at Pentecost, did so by *pouring* out His Spirit upon them. *Pouring* is therefore very clearly described as a biblical mode of *baptism*.

Dipping

Another mode of baptizing in the New Testament is that of dipping. Dipping is sometimes thought of as "quick immersion" but it can also be seen as *partial immersion*. In two of the accounts of the Last Supper, we see it used in this way. The word that is used in these passages is *bapto*, a word related closely to *baptizo*—and both words can refer to the partial immersion of dipping. "He answered and said, 'He who dipped his *hand* with Me in the dish will betray Me' (Matt. 26:23). The apostle John says something similar. "Jesus answered, 'It is he to whom I shall give *a piece of bread* when I have dipped it.' And having dipped the bread, He gave it to Judas Iscariot, the son of Simon" (John 13:26).

It is clear contextually in both these usages that total immersion is not in view. When a dip for food is used at a meal it has never been customary to immerse one's entire *hand* in the dish as Matthew describes. Nor has it been the practice to submerge the *food* entirely in the dip as John describes. The context therefore makes it plain that this dipping was a partial immersion, not a total immersion. And though we have all seen people immerse chips in salsa, we have probably not seen it done on purpose.

Identification

Baptism also is used to refer to a complete identification. In 1 Corinthians 10, there is an apparent metaphorical use of the word *baptize*, without any reference to the baptized going down into the water or the water coming down upon the baptized.

> Moreover, brethren, I do not want you to be unaware that all our fathers were under the cloud, all passed through the sea, all were baptized into Moses in the cloud and in

the sea, all ate the same spiritual food, and all drank the same spiritual drink. For they drank of that spiritual Rock that followed them, and that Rock was Christ (1 Cor. 10:1-4).

Those familiar with the story of the Red Sea crossing will remember that the whole point of this remarkable deliverance was that the Israelites did not get wet at all. It was the Egyptians who were immersed. Nevertheless, although the Israelites remained dry, they were still *baptized* into Moses. The contextual meaning does not seem to be that they were immersed into Moses, but rather that they were formally *identified* with him. After the Red Sea, their identity was found in Moses, and they were committed to follow him.

Immersion/Pouring and Sprinkling

We can also see how various modes of baptism work together. The last "mode" of baptizing we will consider is that of immersion/pouring and sprinkling together.

Just as the Lord's Supper grew out of the Passover, but is certainly distinct from it, so Christian baptism grew out of the Old Testament washings and purifications. These washings are called *baptisms* in the New Testament (Heb. 9:9-10). It is this that perhaps has created misunderstanding—there is a common belief that the ceremonial cleansings of the Old Testament were always accomplished through sprinklings *alone*. Sprinklings were certainly involved, but so was bathing and washing—which perhaps involved immersion.

For example, consider Numbers 19. The chapter contains *sprinkling* with blood (v. 4), *sprinkling* with the water of purification (vv. 13 & 20), which was most likely sprinkling with ashes from the heifer (vv. 17-19). But this chapter in Numbers also teaches that the person who was unclean and was sprinkled in this way must *complete* his cleansing on the seventh day by *bathing in water* (v. 19). In other words, he is first sprinkled, and then washes much more thoroughly—he is immersed, or water is poured on him.

Why is he sprinkled? The probable answer to this question shows the necessity of a subsequent immersion. In Hebrews 9:13, in reference to Numbers 19, we are taught that when the ashes of the heifer were *sprinkled* on the unclean, it resulted in a purification of the flesh. It was an *external* cleansing. These ashes produced a physical purity. It included what Christian baptism does not—a removal of dirt from the body. But how can this be accomplished by the ashes of a heifer? It is significant that the sacrifice of the heifer provided the Israelites with the two main ingredients of *soap*. There was the fat from the heifer, and there was ash from cedar wood that was burned on the altar along with the heifer (v. 6). Animal tallow and wood ash can be used to make soap. This soap was sprinkled on the Israelites, and was followed up by a washing bath. In the Passover, certain elements were dropped when the Lord's supper was instituted, and those elements which remained retained a much richer spiritual signification. So with baptism. Certain accompanying practices (such as the soap) have dropped away from the ceremonies of purification.

Another change was the *repetitive* nature of the purifying baths. Just as they had to sacrifice again and again in the Old Covenant, so they had to wash again and again. But because Christ has appeared as our once-for-all sacrifice, it is no longer necessary for us to bathe again and again. And the one immersion that is performed is *not* to be understood as a bath, or physical cleansing (1 Pet. 3:21). Peter's disclaimer that baptism is not a washing of dirt from the body shows that the ceremonial washings of the Old Covenant were still very much in view, at least in the minds of some. Peter has to warn them that Christian baptism is not an external washing, as the baptisms of Numbers 19 were. In the same way the author of

Hebrews contrasts what the ashes of a heifer do (cleanse someone *outwardly*) with what the blood of Christ does (cleanse someone *inwardly*).

Ceremonial Cleansing

With this in view, we can now see the connection between these ceremonial washings of Numbers 19 and the word *baptism* in the discussion of Hebrews 9. "It was symbolic for the present time in which both gifts and sacrifices are offered which cannot make him who performed the service perfect in regard to the conscience—concerned only with foods and drinks, various washings, and fleshly ordinances imposed until the time of reformation" (Heb. 9:9-10). The translation here *various washings* is literally *various baptisms*. The author of Hebrews then goes on to discuss these various baptisms.

> For if the blood of bulls and goats and the ashes of a heifer, sprinkling the unclean, sanctifies for the purifying of the flesh, how much more shall the blood of Christ, who through the eternal Spirit offered Himself without spot to God, cleanse your conscience from dead works to serve the living God? (Heb. 9:13-14)

In other words, the sprinkling of the ashes of the heifer is included in his discussion of the various baptisms of the Old Covenant. We see in Numbers that this also involved *washing*, or bathing, but we see in Hebrews that it also involved *sprinkling*. We commonly make a mistake about sprinkling because when we think of "ceremonial cleansing" we think of modern liturgical ceremonies—a priest sprinkles with holy water and declares the person somehow mysteriously and invisibly "clean." But in contrast to this conception of ceremonial cleanliness, the Jewish ceremonies *killed germs*. They used soap and water. And obviously, it is very likely that the way they washed when they came to bathe after the sprinkling was through pouring, or immersion. Both actions are completely natural in washing. We do the same today with showers (pouring) and baths (immersion).

In Mark 7, we are informed that the Jews took the whole process of baptizing very seriously—they even would wash (literally, *baptize*) cups, pitchers, copper vessels, and *couches*. This was done in what was called a *miqvah*. It was a small pool with steps down into it. Forty-eight such *miqvahs* have been excavated by archeologists in the area of the Temple at Jerusalem, but private homes also contained them. But even with a *miqvah*, it seems obvious the baptism of couches would most likely have been accomplished through some means other than immersion.

The water that Jesus turned to wine at Cana was water that was used in such ceremonial cleansings. The amount of water involved certainly demonstrates that we are not dealing with a few sprinkled drops of water alone. "Now there were set there six waterpots of stone, according to the manner of purification of the Jews, containing twenty or thirty gallons apiece" (John 2:6). For purposes of comparison, this is about the same as what two or three fifty-gallon drums would hold. Obviously, it was enough water to fill a modern bathtub.

Burial Imagery

The foregoing should make it clear that immersion should also be accepted as a biblical mode of baptism. In Romans 6, we see the word *baptism* referred to in a sense which is at least consistent with the practice of immersion. "Or do you not know that as many of us as were baptized into Christ Jesus were baptized into His death? Therefore we were buried with Him through baptism into death, that just as Christ was raised from the dead by the glory of the Father, even so we also should walk in newness of life" (Rom. 6:3-4). Paul here says that we Christians were *buried* with Christ through baptism.

While it is true that water is not mentioned in this passage, it is clear that water baptism is connected to the spiritual reality of the Spirit's baptism. One such reality that may be in view in baptism is that of burial. When someone is buried they are completely enclosed or surrounded. In the same way, when someone is immersed in water, he is completely enclosed or surrounded. When we consider the lexical evidence (i.e. that one of the meanings of *baptize* is *immerse*), and we see that Paul uses the imagery of burial in association with baptism, it appears fair to say immersion is at least consistent with the scriptural teaching of baptism. At the same time, care must be taken to avoid imposing modern burial habits on an ancient text. The way we baptize by immersion (lowering into the water) and the way we bury (lowering into the ground) do appear similar. This similarity, however, disappears when we remember that Jesus was buried through being enclosed in a small room with a door.

The fact that our union with Christ is stated in Romans as a burial cannot dictate to us that immersion is the *sine qua non* of baptism. Elsewhere Paul makes the same point about our union with Christ, and our baptism, but uses a completely different figure, that of putting on an article of clothing. "For as many of you as were baptized into Christ have *put on* Christ" (Gal. 3:27). So we must be careful not to impose a certain choreography on baptism. The ordinance is not to be considered as a replication, or dramatic reenactment, of Christ's sufferings. The key thought is union with Christ, and identification with Him. This can be done equally well through pouring, immersion, or sprinkling. Provided that baptism with water is administered in the name of the Father, Son, and Holy Spirit, and administered within the boundaries of the Christian faith, there is ample scriptural grounds for accepting *all* these modes as valid biblical forms of baptism.

10

Exclusive Immersion?

Defining the Debate

Even though the mode of baptism is one of the least important things about it, likemindedness between Christians on the subject is one of the *most* important things about it. Consequently, it may be wise to take a more detailed look at this aspect of the debate. Surprisingly for some, this facet of the baptism debate is the easiest to settle from the Word. Can the claim be sustained that immersion is the only form of baptism recognized by the Word? In the section that follows, some points made earlier will be repeated. However, the purpose here is to argue against the exclusivity of immersion and not, as earlier, simply to set forth the modes of baptism as described in Scripture. Even so, no challenge is being made here to the propriety of immersion as biblical baptism. I am seeking to critique the *exclusive* immersionist position, showing that pouring and sprinkling are also appropriate.

The words concerned are *bapto* and *baptizo*. The classical Baptist position was summarized by Dale as follows:

1. *Baptizo*, throughout all Greek literature, has only one meaning, and that meaning is clear and precise.

2. *Baptizo* and *bapto* have exactly the same meaning, with the solitary exception of "dyeing."

3. *Baptizo* expresses a definite act or mode, and that is, "to dip."

4. *Baptizo* means the same thing in figurative and literal usage.

It is commonly assumed that these convictions about immersion are supported by the Greek lexicons. However, Dr. Carson, the great 19th century Baptist apologist, had this to say. "My position is, that it always signifies to dip; never expressing anything but mode. Now, as *I have all the lexicographers and commentators against me* in this opinion, it will be necessary to say a word or two with respect to the authority of lexicons." [Emphasis mine] The counterexamples are many; below are just some samples.

Dr. Carson's claim that "it always signifies to dip" is not true in classical Greek (Aristotle, *Hist. Anim.* v, 15). It is not true in Judaic Greek (LXX: Dan. 4:33). It is not true in New Testament Greek (Matt. 26:23; Heb. 9:10). In short, the claim of exclusivity for immersion is demonstrably *not true*. The commitment to "just one mode" is *not* required by the historical usage of the words. Greek lexicons are simply the record of these historical usages.

Three Considerations

It is often thought that Romans 6, with its teaching on burial with Christ in baptism, requires immersion in all cases. The image of burial is certainly in this passage, as well as the *possible* idea of *immersion*. But there are three considerations here against using this to show *immersion* as the exclusive use of the word. First, the debate is not between immersionists and anti-immersionists. It is between "*exclusive* immersionists" and "open immersionists." Consequently, to show a case of immersion in Scripture shows nothing one way or the other.

Secondly, there are counterexamples. Other images are used with regard to baptism as well (Col. 2:11-12). Take, for example, the image cited earlier of getting dressed: "For as many of you as were baptized into Christ have put on Christ" (Gal. 3:27). And last, Christ was not buried in the same manner as we are buried. Our baptisms by immersion are not, therefore, an accurate "reenactment" of Christ's burial. But scripturally, they do not have to be.

Our concern as Christians should be how the Bible uses *bapto* and *baptizo*. We see pouring in Acts 1:5, Acts 11:15-16, and Acts 2:17. We see partial immersion in Matthew 26:23 and John 13:26. We see complete identification in 1 Corinthians 10:1-4. We see sprinkling when we compare Hebrews 9:9-10 with Numbers 19:4,13,17-20, and then look at Hebrews 9:13-14. The word translated "washings" is the noun *baptismos*. The Old Testament washings and sprinklings are described by the author of Hebrews as *baptisms*: "concerned only with foods and drinks, *various washings*, and fleshly ordinances imposed until the time of reformation. . . . For if the blood of bulls and goats and the ashes of a heifer, *sprinkling the unclean*, sanctifies for the purifying of the flesh" (Heb. 9:10,13). And lastly, we see the possibility of immersion in *one* of the basic lexical meanings of the word, as well as a possible hint in the burial with Christ taught in Romans 6.

Sprinkling With Water

We see indications of the mode of baptism in the Old Testament. "So shall He *sprinkle* many nations. Kings shall shut their mouths at Him; for what had not been told them they shall see, and what they had not heard they shall consider" (Is. 52:15). The Ethiopian eunuch was reading within six verses of this passage of Scripture when Philip approached him. A short time later, the eunuch, from one of many nations spoken of, was requesting *baptism*. And speaking of the Ethiopian eunuch, the prepositions of Scripture, with reference to water, establish nothing one way or the other. The eunuch went down into the water, and came up out of the water. *But so did Philip.* "So he commanded the chariot to stand still. And *both* Philip and the eunuch *went down into the water,* and he baptized him. Now when *they came up out of the water,* the Spirit of the Lord caught Philip away, so that the eunuch saw him no more; and he went on his way rejoicing" (Acts 8:38-39).

In Isaiah, the times of the new covenant, the coming days of glory, are spoken of in terms of the sprinkling of water. Whether this is an explicit prophecy of baptism or not, it certainly shows the adequacy of sprinkling to picture forgiveness of sins. The same is true in Ezekiel. "Then I will sprinkle clean water on you, and you shall be clean; I will cleanse you from all your filthiness and from all your idols. I will give you a new heart and put a new spirit within you; I will take the heart of stone out of your flesh and give you a heart of flesh" (Ez. 36:25-26).

The Blood of Sprinkling

Sprinkling is also wonderfully associated with the cleansing blood of Christ. The blood of Christ is at the heart of the new covenant. It is therefore not surprising to find this declared in one of the ordinances of the new covenant, the Lord's Supper. "For this is My blood of the new covenant, which is shed for many for the remission of sins" (Matt. 26:28; *cf.* Mark 14:24; Luke 22:20; John 6:53-56; 1 Cor. 10:16; 11:25-27). But is the blood of Christ connected to our *initial* entry into the new covenant? Is it connected to the entry point also marked by baptism? The answer is clearly *yes.*

"Elect according to the foreknowledge of God the Father, in sanctification of the Spirit, for obedience and *sprinkling of the blood of Jesus Christ*: Grace to you and peace be multiplied" (1 Pet. 1:2). And in the book of Hebrews, it says, "To Jesus the Mediator of the new covenant, and to *the blood of sprinkling* that speaks better things than that of Abel" (Heb.

12:24). The author of Hebrews also says, "Therefore not even the first covenant was dedicated without [the sprinkling of] blood" (Heb. 9:18-22). The sprinkling of the blood of Christ is what sets us apart as Christians. Prior to that sprinkling, we have not been cleansed. The blood of the covenant sets us apart, or *sanctifies* us. "Of how much worse punishment, do you suppose, will he be thought worthy who has trampled the Son of God underfoot, counted *the blood of the covenant by which he was sanctified* a common thing, and insulted the Spirit of grace?" (Heb. 10:29). As a better covenant, with better promises (Heb. 8:6), the new covenant also has much greater cursings associated with it (Heb. 2:1-3; 6:1-8; 10:26-31). Nevertheless, the blood of the covenant is seen as something which sets a man apart covenantally. The blood of this covenant was applied through sprinkling. Sprinkling therefore presents a wonderful biblical image of cleansing.

In Hebrews 10, we see the kind of exhortation that older teachers used to call "improving one's baptism." "Let us draw near with a true heart in full assurance of faith, having *our hearts sprinkled* from an evil conscience and our bodies washed with pure water" (Heb. 10:22). This is another reference to the heifer sacrifice of Numbers 19, in which a person was sprinkled, and then he would go on to wash. The entire image is applied to all believers in Christ.

Baptism is certainly connected to our cleansing from sin. "And now why are you waiting? Arise and be *baptized*, and *wash away your sins*, calling on the name of the Lord" (Acts 22:16). But we are also cleansed by the sprinkling of the blood of Christ. "How much more shall *the blood of Christ*, who through the eternal Spirit offered Himself without spot to God, *cleanse your conscience* from dead works to serve the living God?" (Heb. 9:14) The apostle John also teaches the same. "But if we walk in the light as He is in the light, we have fellowship with one another, and *the blood of Jesus Christ* His

Son *cleanses* us from all sin" (1 John 1:7; cf. Rev. 1:5). And Scripture uniformly describes the mode of this initial cleansing from sin through the blood of Christ as that of *sprinkling*.

When the foregoing is carefully considered, it may safely be said that claims of exclusivity for immersion cannot be biblically defended. A case for immersion as *a* biblical mode can be made from Scripture, but to say that it is *the* biblical mode cannot be sustained.

11

The Everlasting Covenant: A Summary

Confirmed to Abraham

Near the beginning of our redemptive history, the Lord God came to Abraham and graciously made an *everlasting* covenant with him (Gen. 17:7,13). God, who cannot lie or change, sealed this covenant with Abraham in an oath, taken in His own name, so that *believers throughout all history* might have strong consolation (Heb. 6:18). Since there was no one greater to swear by, God swore to this covenant by Himself, because He had determined to show the heirs of promise that this everlasting covenant was indeed *everlasting*, and that His counsel in this matter was *immutable* (Heb. 6:13-14, 17-18). This covenant with Abraham, confirmed to him *in Christ*, was a covenant which by its very nature could not be annulled (Gal. 3:17). We can see how God has fulfilled His promise to Abraham; it is by the blood of this everlasting covenant that we as Christians are saved (Heb. 13:20). The covenant made with Abraham is still in force today; this glorious covenant made with Abraham millennia ago is nothing other than the *new* covenant.

God's Gracious Promise

Abraham was commanded by God to place the sign of this covenant upon the male *infants* of his household (Gen.

17:10). This he did in faith, placing on them a sign of the *promise*, and not of the law (Gal. 3:18). Abraham's physical descendants were required by this to follow in the footsteps of their covenant father, Abraham. This they did, but in two divergent ways (Rom. 9:6-7, 13). Some of them simply mimicked Abraham's *external* actions, showing themselves really to be nothing more than children of the devil (John 8:39,44). They, boasting in their physical lineage from Abraham alone, gathered themselves into assemblies that were actually synagogues of Satan (Rev. 2:9; John 8:39,44).

But others, children of the promise, imitated Abraham's faith, showing themselves to be his true and faithful offspring (Rom. 4:12). The Bible teaches that only those Jews who are of faith are true heirs of the gracious promise to Abraham (Gal. 3:7). A true Jew was the man who was circumcised in his heart (Rom. 2:28-29). The children of the promise, characterized by faith, are those who remain in the covenant *forever* (John 8:35). Because they are elect, they can never fall away from salvation (Rom. 8:33). However, it *is* possible for the non-elect to have covenantal obligations before God, and to fall away from that covenant (Gal. 5:4). These children after the flesh remain in the covenant only for a time, until God judges them for their covenantal disobedience and unbelief (Rom. 11:20). As it was for professing Israel then, so it is for "professing" Christians now (Rom. 11:21). We must remember these warnings, for we Gentiles were grafted into the olive tree of Israel, and are warned that the same judgments may befall us (Rom. 11:26-27).

Sign of the Gospel

On the issue of infant baptism, much confusion is caused by the assumption that the New Covenant set aside everything found in the Old Testament. But the New Testament teaches that there is an important distinction between the *promise* given to Abraham and the *law* given to Moses. Circumcision was the sign of the promise, *i.e.* it was the sign of the *gospel*. When the law of Moses came, hundreds of years after Abraham, it came in partial fulfillment of the covenant with Abraham (Ex. 2:24-25). It was a *temporary* administration of shadows, ceremonies, and types, all designed, when rightly understood, to prepare the way for the fulfillment of the promise to Abraham. Abraham had been shown the blueprints of a great house, and he believed that God would in fact build it (Gal. 3:6,8). Throughout the Old Testament, the house promised to Abraham was in the process of being built, and the Levitical administration of the law was a God-given, but *temporary*, scaffolding designed to aid in the construction of the *everlasting* house (Heb. 8:13). That scaffolding was not ever intended to be a part of the permanent house (Col. 2:16-17). And of course God did not intend to tear down the Abrahamic house when He tore down the Mosaic scaffolding.

Moses understood this, and was a faithful servant in the house of Christ. As the Son was faithful *over* the house, so Moses was a faithful servant *in* the house (Heb. 3:5-6). Moses, we are told, embraced the reproach of serving *Christ* (Heb. 11:24-26). Those who were baptized into the name of Moses were given the tremendous covenantal privilege of drinking from *Christ* in the wilderness (1 Cor. 10:4). Those who had faith were greatly blessed (Heb. 11:29). Those who were blinded by unbelief had their bodies scattered over the wilderness (Heb. 3:16-17; 1 Cor. 10:5). They fell because they had tempted *Christ* (1 Cor. 10:9). For this reason, Christians are to take special care in how they participate in the covenantal meal of the New Covenant (1 Cor. 10:14-16). This is because the Lord of Israel then is the Lord of Israel now, and God is not mocked.

But as the centuries progressed, there were many of Abraham's physical and genetic descendants, blinded by sin, who came to think that as God's chosen and covenant people they had an *automatic* right to the blessings of the covenant (John 8:33). They thought that the Jews were God's people, *period*, and that physical descent from Abraham was alone sufficient to secure their place. But the Word of God stood against them from first to last (Acts 7:51). Our Lord was astonished that a teacher of Israel did not understand that it was absolutely necessary for *Jews* to be born again (John 3:10). God can make sons of Abraham out of rocks (Matt. 3:9), and considering the stone-like hearts of unbelieving Israelites, that is exactly what He did whenever He regenerated any of them (Ez. 11:19).

Root of Jesse

The stock of true Israel has always been the Lord Jesus Christ Himself. He alone is the Root of Jesse (Is. 11:10), the trunk from which all true spiritual fruit grows. But as the tree of Israel grew out from Christ, developing in history, it became increasingly apparent that many of the branches in covenant with Him were fruitless. God solemnly warned them that fruitlessness was *intolerable* (Matt. 3:10; 21:43). They had forgotten their dependence on the Root; in their moral idiocy, they thought that *He* was dependent upon *them* (Rom. 11:18). As is true of all fruitless branches, they had no permanent place on the vine (John 15:6). Because of their unbelief, they were cut away from the olive tree of Israel (Rom. 11:17). We know that nothing can separate a man from God's election to salvation (Rom. 8:29-30). So they were not removed from God's saving decree; they were removed from His *covenant* (Rom. 11:7).

But how had they come *into* this covenant, from which so many of them were now to be removed? The sign of this covenant had been placed on them when they were only eight days old (Gen. 17:12). Prior to the advent of Christ, the vast majority of Jews had come into their covenantal connection with this one olive tree in their *infancy*. They had *grown* on this one tree. And those branches which had borne fruit had, *by faith*, remained on this one tree, while fruitless branches were removed and destined for the fire of judgment. The Gentiles who believed were grafted into *this same tree*. Gentiles were brought in alongside faithful Jews who had been there since *infancy*. God did not plant a new tree; He has been *cultivating the same tree* since the time of Abraham.

Gentile Grafts

In the first century, God began to bring in large numbers of Gentiles, in just the way He had promised to Abraham (Gen. 12:3; Gal. 3:8). Gentiles were now being grafted into the covenanted olive tree of Israel (Rom. 11:17). These Gentiles were grafted in alongside believing Jews who had been there, in that same tree, *since infancy*. While leaving the substance of the covenant itself untouched (we must remember it was an *everlasting* covenant), our sovereign Lord determined that He would alter the *external* sign of the Abrahamic covenant. Before, that sign had been circumcision. Christ now declared that the means of sealing the nations promised to Abraham (Rom. 4:13) was to be accomplished through *baptism* (Matt. 28:19).

Now this new grafting technique of baptism was unsettling to some zealous Jews who had believed in Christ (Acts 15:1). Surely, they thought, the Abrahamic covenant would have to be sealed in circumcision! The apostolic response to this objection was that Gentiles were to be brought into Israel by means of *baptism*. By one Spirit both Jews and Greeks were *baptized* into the body (1 Cor. 12:13). Anyone who was *baptized* into Christ, whether Jew or Greek, had put on Christ (Gal. 3:27-28). And if someone was *baptized* into Christ, then he was an heir to *Abraham's* promise (Gal. 3:29). Baptism was

therefore sufficient for Gentiles; circumcision was unnecessary (Acts 15:24). The middle wall of partition had come down
(Eph. 2:14), and the Gentiles had been brought into the commonwealth of *Israel* by the blood of Christ (Eph. 2:11-13).
They were now one with believing Jews because there was
just one Lord, one faith, and one *baptism* (Eph. 4:5).

The Nature of the Controversy

But this nevertheless resulted in no small controversy
among the saints. Should not the Gentiles be required to come
into Israel the *proper* way—the way that had been practiced
since ancient times? The answer was *no*; circumcision was unnecessary, because *baptism had replaced circumcision as the sign of
the covenant* (Col. 2:11-12). Baptism is the initiatory rite for the
Christian church (Acts 2:41), which is the New Covenant community (2 Cor. 3:6). Baptism is therefore the initiatory rite for
the New *Covenant* community. It is therefore obviously a *covenantal* ordinance.

This ancient controversy among the saints, now long
settled, is still instructive for us today. The Gentiles had been
included with the true Israel (Gal. 6:16). They were now citi-
zens of the Jerusalem above (Gal. 4:26). They had been borne
by the barren woman who was now giving birth to a new
world (Gal. 4:27). But this *inclusion* happened in such a way
that many believing Jews were greatly unsettled by the external change from circumcision to baptism. There was therefore a great controversy over this, one that dominates New
Testament history.

This should make us pause. Suppose the Lord had made
more than just the administrative change from the knife of
circumcision to the water of baptism. Suppose God had de-
creed that under the New Covenant, the people of God, Jew
and Gentile alike, were required to begin *excluding* their new-
born children from the covenant community. No one dis-

putes that the Lord could have done this. No one of us deserves a place in that covenant community; we have no right to demand it, for ourselves *or* for our children. But *if* the Lord had done this, it would have marked a profound and fundamental *change* from how He had dealt with His people from the time of Abraham on. Such a change is conceivable; the Lord made other changes. But whenever He changed the administration of His covenant, *He informed His covenant people of the change.* And even when He informed them of such administrative changes, they were still difficult changes to bring about in the church.

So if the Lord had chosen to make this change of excluding infants from the covenant, He would have taught us on it. And if He *had* taught it, there would have been considerable turmoil throughout the pages of the New Testament in the apostolic attempts to get the saints to understand and accept it. But the New Testament is silent on both counts. According to the baptist understanding, a profound change in the conditions of the covenant was made, a change which *for the very first time* excluded children, without any instruction from God on it, and without a ripple of protest from any professing Christians. But the Bible says that not even human covenants can be changed or added to in such a fashion (Gal. 3:15). The modern supposition that the believers of the first century were so astonishingly docile on such an issue reveals how far removed we are from their covenantal presuppositions. The modern individualistic mindset does not comprehend the critical scriptural importance of faithful *covenantal children*, and faithful *covenantal descendants*.

We can see throughout the New Testament the controversy caused by the *inclusion* of believing but *uncircumcised* Gentiles (Gal. 2:11-12). Where is the controversy caused by the exclusion of the *circumcised* infants of believing Jews? There is *no such controversy*. But is it reasonable to suppose that those who so loudly objected to the *inclusion* of uncircumcised Gentiles would somehow not object at all to the *exclusion* of their own *circumcised* children? Were the saints really being taught that additions to the olive tree were now all to be made by grafting alone, and that no one *grows* on the tree any more? *Not at all* (Rom. 11:17).

Continuity of the Covenant

There is continuity in this everlasting covenant, from Abraham to the present. There is continuity with the people who were created by that covenant, from Abraham to the present. God has said *throughout all Scripture* that He will be our God, and we shall be His people (Ex. 6:7; Lev. 26:12; Jer. 7:23; 11:4; 30:22; Ez. 36:28; Hos. 1:9; Rom. 9:25-26). This is a central promise. There is no reason to believe the New Covenant has made *God's people* childless and barren. The prophets said that spiritual fruitfulness would increase under the New Covenant, not decrease and vanish!

With this contextual understanding, we should turn to consider what parents under the New Covenant are *expressly* taught concerning their covenant children. It is true that the New Covenant nowhere excludes the children of believers. But what are some express indications of their continued and ongoing *inclusion* in the covenant?

The first Christian sermon cut the listeners to the heart. They cried out, seeking what to do. Peter told them to repent and be *baptized*, and that the promise was to them *and to their children* (Acts 2:39). We are taught that children of at least one believing parent are *holy*. The word used by Paul is *hagia*, which when applied to *persons* is almost always translated *saint* (1 Cor. 7:14). Little children and infants are included by Christ in the kingdom of *God* (Luke 18:16). Children constitute one of the recognized subgroups of the church, to be taught along with the rest of the *saints* in the church (Eph. 1:1; 6:1; Col. 1:2;

3:20). Little Gentile children are taught that the *covenant promise* made at Sinai applied to *them*, just as it had to Israelite children from infancy on (Eph. 6:1-3). We are taught that one of the features of the New Covenant was to be the *restoration* of the covenantal father/child relationship, not the dissolution of the covenantal father/child relationship (Luke 1:17). Ephesian children were commanded to obey their parents *in the Lord* (Eph. 6:1).

We also know that, in the New Testament, circumcision continued to be a sign of a true evangelical relationship to God (Rom. 2:29). Christian Jews continued to apply that sign to their infants (Acts 21:21). Such circumcision meant that such children were members of their parents' synagogue, and we know believing Jews assembled in *Christian* synagogues (Jas. 2:2). These were also considered Christian *churches* (Jas. 5:14). Therefore we *know* that certain first-century churches had infant members.

The gospel, we are taught, is for the *families* of the earth (Acts 3:25). It is therefore not surprising that the normal mode of evangelism and baptism in the New Testament was household by household (Acts 16:14-15). The point is not that such are narratives of infant baptisms. The point is that they are narratives of *household* or *family* baptisms (1 Cor. 1:16).

And last, one of the most precious doctrines of Scripture for believing parents is the teaching of *covenantal succession* from one generation to the next (Ps. 102:28). Faithful parents are promised that their children will follow the Lord (Dt. 7:9). Moreover, the blessings of this covenantal succession were prophesied as coming into a glorious fulfillment under the New Covenant (Ez. 37:24-26; Is. 59:21; 65:23; Jer. 32:38-40). The responsibility for the reverence and faithfulness of children is therefore quite properly delegated to parents (Eph. 6:4; 1 Tim. 3:4; Titus 1:6). Under the New Covenant, our children's children are truly *included* (Ps. 103; Luke 1:48-50).